Texas A&M University Press
publishing since 1974

More Historic Homes of Waco, Texas

Publication of this book was assisted in part by generous funding
from the Summerlee Foundation of Dallas

More Historic Homes of Waco, Texas

Kenneth Hafertepe

Texas A&M University Press
College Station

∞ This paper meets the requirements of ANSI/NISO Z39.48-1992 (Permanence of Paper).
Binding materials have been chosen for durability.
Manufactured in China through Martin Book Management

Unless otherwise noted, all photographs are by author.

Library of Congress Cataloging-in-Publication Data

Names: Hafertepe, Kenneth, 1955– author.
Title: More historic homes of Waco, Texas / Kenneth Hafertepe.
Description: First edition. | College Station: Texas A&M University Press,
  [2024] | Includes bibliographical references and index.
Identifiers: LCCN 2023041882 (print) | LCCN 2023041883 (ebook) | ISBN
  9781648431180 (cloth) | ISBN 9781648431197 (ebook)
Subjects: LCSH: Historic buildings—Texas—Waco. | Waco (Tex.)—Buildings,
  structures, etc. | BISAC: ARCHITECTURE / Historic Preservation / General
  | HISTORY / United States / State & Local / Southwest (AZ, NM, OK, TX)
Classification: LCC F394.W12 H26 2024 (print) | LCC F394.W12 (ebook) |
  DDC 976.4/284—dc23/eng/20230913
LC record available at https://lccn.loc.gov/2023041882
LC ebook record available at https://lccn.loc.gov/2023041883

CONTENTS

ACKNOWLEDGMENTS

IN THE PROCESS of writing a book about the *Historic Homes of Waco, Texas*, I began to realize that there needed to be a book about the historic buildings of Waco that were not houses; this resulted in a volume that appeared in 2023, *Historic Buildings of Waco, Texas*. But as I wrote that book, I realized that there were many other houses that had intriguing stories—hence the book that you are examining. One might assume that these historic houses were ones that did not make the cut into *Historic Homes*, but actually many of these were ones that I did not know enough about to include there. Which is to say that working on historic Waco has been a life-long learning opportunity, the kind I enjoy pursuing.

Once again, I am indebted to institutions and to individuals in Waco and beyond for what you are about to read. The Texas Collection at Baylor University is still my home library and my happy place. In the previous volumes I thanked former directors Kent Keeth, Tom Charlton, and John Wilson, and I am happy to report that there is a new sheriff at the Texas Collection, Jeff Pirtle, who is providing new energy and steady leadership. The digital resources continue to expand, which has made it even easier to utilize the treasures of the Texas Collection. Other internet sources continue to be incredibly helpful, notably Heritage Quest, newspapers.com, Find-a-Grave.com, and especially the Portal to Texas History.

Another treasure trove is the Institute for Oral History at Baylor, the brainchild of Thomas Charlton, then nurtured by Rebecca Sharpless and now by Stephen Sloan. These remarkable resources, many of which are now available online, include recordings of interviews with Lavonia Jenkins Barnes, whom I never met, and Eb Morrow, whom I knew when he lived across the street from me, which was especially helpful because it reminded me of things that Eb told me twenty years ago that I had forgotten.

My local brain trust is still incredibly supportive: in alphabetical order this includes Eric Ames, Willis T. Bradford, Don Davis, and B. J. Greaves. They have now been joined by Clint Lynch of Oakwood Cemetery and Sean Sutcliffe of the Waco McLennan County Library, who were especially helpful in tracking down divorced Camerons. However, any error in this book is on me, not them.

In returning to a study of domestic structures, I am once again beholden to many homeowners both past and present. I met Gigi Bowie while we were both serving on the City of Waco's Historic Landmark Preservation Commission (HLPC), and we have remained friends. She kindly showed me around the Butler-Harrison house in East Waco. The ever-energetic Nancy Grayson has been a leader in the revitalization of East Waco, including her restoration of both 210 Peach Street and 176 Pecan Street, and was happy to show me around both of them.

Yet another HLPC friend, Erin B. Shank, showed me the William and Jennie Colgin house on Lower Austin Avenue, which she and her husband, John Shank, have restored. Randy Lane not only showed me through the Sanford-Barrett house but also interviewed me for the Waco History Podcast along with our friend Stephen Sloan. And Missy Morris was gracious enough to talk with a strange man about the house she worked in (the Elton and Maude Hunter house) and to let him take a look around the first floor.

A third friend from the HLPC, Mary Helen George, showed me around the Mrs. Hattie Richards house, which she and her husband, David George, have lovingly maintained. Next door to David and Mary Helen, Carolyn Doolittle showed me through the Fentress-Hoehn house. Also in Castle Heights Sam and Becky Griffin have done a nice job of keeping up the Wallerstedt house, and Becky was kind enough to let me check out the interior. My Baylor colleague Elesha Coffman was kind enough to show me the Charles and Millicent Caldwell house, a.k.a. the Presbyterian Manse, which is one of the gems of the Karem Park Addition.

Rick and Alice Anne Brunn welcomed me to the Chambers-Murphy-Kendrick house, one of the most elegant in Dean Highlands. Richard and Carrin Ellis have provided information and historic photos about the Valentine and Kathleen Cox house. And in Lower Dean Highlands (does such a place exist?) my real estate pal Barbie Dutton went through the George and Adele Bashara house with me. As is so often the case, I was lucky it was for sale.

Wacoans are a very neighborly sort, and that is especially true in my neighborhood, Sanger Heights, where I have lived for twenty-three years. In fact, my Baylor colleague Laine Scales has created the Good Neighbor House from the Sinclair-Sarratt house. Another Baylor colleague, Dan Walden, showed me the Webb-Johnson house. My friends Bland Schwarting and Joe Herrera have done a remarkable job of bringing the Richard and Mary Munroe house back to its early appearance and have shared cool old photos of the house. If Bland finds any more historical information, he may have to write a book about Sanger Heights.

Even newer and nearer neighbors, Rory and Alexa Partin, discovered one of the architects' drawings for the remodel of the Durham-Morrow house and texted it to me; I am sure that the former owner, Eb Morrow, would be as pleased as I was. And my next-door neighbors, Hilary and David Walker, welcomed me into their home; their son and daughter, Gabriel and Ada, helped their mom with the tour.

Shortly before Wilton A. Lanning Jr. passed away, I had a lovely phone chat with him about the house that his parents built on upper Austin Avenue and other Spencer family houses; my Baylor colleague Heidi Hornik, who later owned that house, informed me that she had found the blueprints and framed one of them, which was incredibly helpful. Henry Wright, a grandson of the architect J. Walter Cocke, provided photos of blueprints of the Harry and Sadie Kestner house, which were tremendously helpful.

Kim Patterson, executive director of the McLennan Community College Foundation, invited me to discuss the future of the Cameron summer residence with other interested Wacoans, which allowed me to see the interior of the house for the first time since it became Art Center Waco. I have been in the Johnson-Taylor house many times over the years, thanks to Kathy and Greg Riggs, Claude Barron, and Jill Barrow, and now Erik Swanson, Georgia Crowhurst, and my sister, Karen Hafertepe.

Once again the Summerlee Foundation has guaranteed that this book would be richly illustrated. Thanks to John Crain, Ron Tyler, and Gary Smith for their encouragement for this project, both moral and financial.

The pandemic slowed down the process of publication, but as you see, it did not kill it. This is a testament to the determination of the staff of Texas A&M University Press to soldier on. Great thanks to Jay Dew, Thom Lemmons, Katie Duelm, and the whole staff, and to copyeditor Cynthia Lindlof, who keeps me consistent and sometimes even grammatical.

When I started these acknowledgments, I thought they would be three paragraphs and a cloud of thanks. Actually writing them had driven home how many people have helped me in this endeavor. To all, *muchas gracias*!

More Historic Homes of Waco, Texas

INTRODUCTION

THIS BOOK IS A continuation of the work I began in *Historic Homes of Waco, Texas*, which was written to make readers—especially Waco readers but also broader audiences—aware of the historic character of Waco houses. I felt that this was especially important in an era when people were buying old houses and fixing them up, because they so often seem to have no clue about what characteristics were historically significant. I saw it as a guide to appreciating everyday architecture and a homily to historic preservation.

On top of that my fellow researcher Stephen Fox had pointed out to me a wonderful resource, the *Texas General Contractors Association Monthly Bulletin*, which listed a large number of building projects, including their architects and contractors, from the 1920s and 1930s. Several days at the Metropolitan Research Center of the Houston Public Library poring through this bulletin left me with a list of Waco buildings and architects unlike anything known, much less published.

Previous to the publication of my first book, the only well-known Waco architects were W. W. Larmour, Roy E. Lane, and Milton W. Scott. The latter was the best documented, thanks to B. J. Greaves and Mildred G. Walker, the authors of the brief but incredibly useful *Milton W. Scott's Waco*. In that first volume I was able to introduce several other Waco architects who had been forgotten: Samuel P. Herbert, T. Brooks Pearson, James P. Baugh, Duke Lovell, Herman F. Cason, E. McIver Ross, and especially Birch D. Easterwood. The first book included nineteen houses by Easterwood, who is mainly remembered as the architect of many Baylor buildings. Since the publication of *Historic Homes* blueprints have come to light that prove he also designed the Hilton and Louise Howell house, which is No. 117 in that book, making an even twenty Easterwood houses. We now have a much better picture of the architects who made Waco houses look the way they do.

As I began working on the first Waco book, I was aware that most of the houses that I was investigating were among the most expensive of their time. In a sense that was inevitable, as the largest and best-built houses tend to be the ones to survive. However, I believed (and still do) that a book like mine should make a very serious attempt to look like the entirety of Waco, not just its better neighborhoods. I hoped that it would include houses of African Americans and Mexican Americans and houses not just of the upper-middle class and upper class but also working-class houses.

Historic Homes included a number of houses owned or occupied by African Americans, even though the largest African American neighborhood was swept away by urban renewal and replaced by housing projects. In spite of that I was able to find a variety of houses with African

American histories, including the two-story house of the leading African American doctor in Waco, the Victorian cottage of a laborer at a local lumber mill, and the bungalow of an East Waco carpenter. I was also able to include four of the remaining shotgun houses, which are generally associated with African Americans. My findings here were surprising: while some were occupied by African Americans, others were originally occupied by poor white people or immigrants. Scholars generally interpret shotguns as reflecting African roots, but the evidence from Waco, fragmentary as it is, suggests that the shotgun is more of an artifact of class than race.

I was less successful finding early houses for Mexican immigrants. This was not for lack of trying, but Mexicans did not begin arriving in Waco until the 1910s and 1920s, fleeing the tumult in their mother country. Most arrived penniless and lived where they could. For many this was the neighborhood that had, until recently, been known as the Reservation, Waco's zone for legalized prostitution. This had been closed so that Waco could have an army camp in the run-up to World War I. What had been North Second Street became "Calle Dos." Alas, this neighborhood of small houses has been cleared away. The only remnant is the monumental St. Francis on the Brazos Catholic Church, specifically planned for the Mexican community in the late 1920s and modeled on Mission San José in San Antonio, a marker of Texas' Hispanic past. (This church is discussed in *Historic Buildings of Waco, Texas*.)

The typical generalization of Waco is that it was settled by people from the Deep South. This may have been true for the first couple of decades, but another thing that was revealed as I surveyed Waco houses beyond the well-known mansions were the contributions of immigrants. Wacoans came from Germany, Poland, Russia, Italy, Sweden, and Canada, as well as from Ohio, New York, Massachusetts, West Virginia, Illinois, Iowa, Nebraska, Missouri, and Washington State. Moreover, Wacoans came from many Southern states, not just the Deep South. The Upland South—Tennessee and Kentucky—was especially well represented. Although Wacoans came from a much more diverse set of localities than just the Deep South, the white and immigrant populations largely chose not to contest the racial realities of Jim Crow no matter where they came from.

The first book also offered a window into the houses of those beyond the well-to-do. Many of the occupations of homeowners in this book are typical of those whose houses are found in city surveys or other architectural studies: doctor, lawyer, banker, insurance broker, stockbroker, cotton broker, newspaper publisher, and auto dealer; owner of a lumberyard, ice factory, wholesale grocery, or wholesale hardware; and maker of drugs, soft drinks, iron products or tents, awnings, and tarpaulins. However, this book goes into new territory in considering the homes of many middle-class and working-class people. Occupations include middle manager, college professor, florist, small restaurant owner, retail grocer, dry goods merchant, motorcycle policeman, salesclerk, traveling salesman, janitor, owner of a cigar and tobacco shop, maker of art glass, draftsman at a cabinetmaking company, and supervisor of a New Deal community center.

My intent in *Historic Homes* was to facilitate the drawing of comparisons across lines of race and class. Perhaps I left too much responsibility in the hands of the readers. It will shock no one that the houses of the working class and of African Americans were smaller and less ornamented than those of Wacoans with more money and/or access to credit. And the surviving houses are probably among the better-built ones, reminding us that much housing of the time was substandard.

Yet the surviving houses also reveal the determination of African Americans, immigrants, and working-class Anglo-Americans to better their lot. Dr. George Conner is a remarkable instance: he not only built himself a substantial two-story house near the Cotton Palace fairground, but he also owned a number of rent houses, some of which were three-room shotgun houses. John and Nettie Kirk, educators at the high school and collegiate levels, built a unique version of a bungalow, with one large gable in front and shed dormers on each side of the roof. Their neighbor, the carpenter Horace Randle, built his own side-gable bungalow a few years later. And Samuel Johnson, a laborer at a local lumberyard, was in a position to observe the latest fashions in Waco house design and incorporate them in his own stylish Victorian home across from Paul Quinn College.

Historic Homes also shed new light on the immigrant experience in Waco. In the last quarter of the nineteenth century, many Jewish people came to Waco from eastern Germany, Poland, and Russia. The remaining houses testify to the increasing success of these immigrants: Jacob and Sarah Levinski, who ran a jewelry store along with their children, built a charming Victorian cottage in the late 1880s in a newer neighborhood on the edge of town. Ambitious young merchants Isaac Goldstein and Louey Migel built similar houses near their synagogue; their success led Isaac and his wife, Jeanie, to build a two-story late-Victorian house around 1904, which was impressive enough to inspire emulation from wholesale grocer Madison Cooper Sr. Louey and his wife, Rebeccah, remained in their cottage for another two decades before buying the palatial (by comparison) Smith-Parker house, where they lived out their lives. Not all Jewish immigrants soared to such heights, but they could still live stylishly, albeit on a smaller scale. Brothers Leo and Edmund Bruck lived in cottages on adjoining lots, a colonial cottage designed by Birch Easterwood and a Tudor cottage by Herman F. Cason. Easterwood also designed a more imposing Italianate house in Castle Heights for merchant Ike Kestner.

Like the African American carpenter Horace Randle, some immigrants were able to live better because they could build their own house. It is well-known that Anglo American brickmakers such as John Wesley Mann and James N. Harris were able to build well because they created their own materials; the German immigrant carpenter Conrad P. Schneider was able to build his own Victorian dream house of wood, which was comparable to cottages designed by the architect W. W. Larmour. This house was later home to immigrants from Italy, Joe and Romelia Pinto. Another immigrant from Italy, Mariano Losavio, bought a recently built frame house with bungalow and foursquare features; in *Historic Buildings of Waco, Texas*, we saw the remarkable Art Deco grocery store that he built on Austin Avenue. At a later date, Christian Mailander, the founder of a business that made display cabinets for stores, lived in a retirement cottage that blended the late Victorian with a bit of the Spanish Colonial.

Waco has also been the home of a number of remarkable women; many were featured in *Historic Homes*. Eliza Earle, the widow of Baylis Wood Earle, became the largest slaveholder in McLennan County at the time of the 1860 census. Though this was quite unusual, it reminds us that wealthy women in Waco and elsewhere were complicit in the American system of slavery, which is now acknowledged as America's original sin. Sarah Levinski was known to most of the employees at the Levinski jewelry store as "Mom" and later became vice president; she and husband, Jake, also were proprietors of the Natatorium Hotel for a while. In the 1920s Lulu Boyd, the widow of Abner Boyd, lived in a simple bungalow while working at Goldstein-Migel Department Store, sometimes as a salesclerk, sometimes as a buyer, and sometimes as a department manager. Her household also included an unmarried son, a widowed daughter, and two grandchildren.

The gulf between Eliza Earle and Lulu Boyd is quite dramatic, but other Waco women were able to wield a power proportionate to Eliza's. Sallie Proctor McLendon, the widow of Jesse Sumpter McLendon, who had founded a retail and wholesale hardware business, long outlived her husband. Remarkably, she decided to leave their old Victorian home near the site of the new Presbyterian church at Austin and Eleventh and build a Colonial Revival house at 2912 Austin, designed by Birch Easterwood. Nor was she the only widow on the upper avenue: Effie Barron, the widow of small-town merchant and banker William Barron, moved to Waco nearly a decade after his death in 1918. As a newcomer to Waco she did not feel compelled to hire a local architect and brought in Bertram C. Hill from Dallas. But women who were less well-off also had a stake in building well: Aura Tanner Hooker was not only the wife of a bank teller but also a seamstress who fashioned many a Cotton Palace gown from the workshop that architect Birch Easterwood incorporated in their Spanish Colonial Revival house on Colcord Avenue.

The houses featured in this new book do not change the broad pattern of Waco houses discussed in *Historic Homes*; however, these additional eighty-eight houses serve to enrich the story. This book continues to identify and discuss the houses of people whose occupations have never been deemed worthy of discussion by architectural historians. In these pages you will find the homes of saloon keepers, horse traders, saddlers, ministers, bookkeepers, candy store owners, piano tuners, and laborers, as well as a few additional doctors, lawyers, lumberyard owners, and the like.

The story of the Sterling family highlights the determination of a multigenerational African American family to make a good home for themselves. The family consisted of Thomas and Emma Sterling; their daughter, Martha, and her husband, George Allen; and their two children. Martha kept house while raising her children, which allowed the other three adults to earn income: Thomas as a custodian at city hall and the police department, George as a porter at Sanger Brothers dry goods store, and Emma as a seamstress. They also rented out rooms to boarders. Out of all this effort they were able to build a large one-story house that fit quite well with the fashion of the first decade of the twentieth century.

A slightly later Foursquare in East Waco shows African American couples following a similar strategy, in which both husband and wife had to be a productive partner. The first occupants of this rent house were J. Michael Buford, a laborer for the nearby Exporters & Traders Compress & Warehouse Company, and his wife, Clara, who kept house but was also a seamstress. They were followed in 1921 by Mitchell and Alberta Fair; Mitchell was a porter at the McLendon Hardware Company in downtown Waco, while Alberta was a "hair culturist," which meant that she sold the products of Madam C. J. Walker, who earned a fortune making and marketing beauty products designed specifically for African American women. And nearby on Taylor Street Jesse and Emma Harrison took a small Victorian house previously owned by white Wacoans and enlarged it to two stories. Again, both husband and wife worked: Jesse was a porter first for a cigar company and then for Cooper Grocery, while Emma was the health supervisor for Waco's "colored" schools.

Some houses alternated between white and black occupants. The little three-room house at 618 S. Twelfth was originally occupied by the Cahill family; Pat was an Anglo-Irish immigrant and saloon keeper. After a few years his family moved to a slightly larger Victorian house on Tenth Street. One African American occupant was Abraham B. Jackson, who worked as the gardener for the Cameron family at their grand Victorian house on Austin Avenue. Another was Ella Walker, who was the cook for the Bush family on Austin. She apparently bought the house and at times lived with the Bush family and rented out the house, an example of a black woman's entrepreneurial spirit.

The pace of immigration to Waco slowed, especially after the US Congress placed new restrictions on immigration in the 1920s. Among those who had immigrated earlier were Norwegians such as Gustav "Gus" Olson, who built many of the most imposing Waco houses of the 1920s, and John E. Johnson, who built the Hilton Hotel, Waco Hall on the Baylor campus, and the McDermott Motor Company. Johnson ended up living in a large and comfortable Foursquare on Colcord Avenue built for the Spencer family.

Another Foursquare—this one on Austin Avenue—was built for an immigrant from Belarus (a.k.a. "Little Russia"), Dave Hawtof, who ran a dry goods store. Hawtof was Jewish, as was Harry Kestner, a merchant and brother of Ike Kestner. Around 1936 Harry and his wife, Sadie, built a Mediterranean Revival house in Castle Heights, which soon became the scene for tea parties to raise funds to send German-Jewish children to Palestine for two years of vocational training.

Also continuing to build were earlier emigrants from the Middle East, especially the Fadal and Bashara families. Both of these families started with fairly conventional bungalows at a time when they were becoming old-fashioned. However, a second generation embraced the more fashionable period cottages, including the one where the Fadal family hosted the young rockabilly singer Elvis Presley, as was recounted in *Historic Homes*. Perhaps the pinnacle of house building for the Bashara family came in 1951, with a Mediterranean villa on Colcord Avenue. This house was built with two cedars of Lebanon framing the entrance, perhaps a nod to their Middle Eastern heritage.

When women were married and not working outside the home, it becomes challenging to evaluate their role in the story. In the first book widows such as Eliza Earle and Effie Cannon Barron were more visible after the death of their husbands, especially Effie, who moved to Waco on her own and chose the architect to design her house. The visibility of widows continues in *Historic Buildings* with Mettie Fisher, whose husband died just as their son was entering Baylor. Mettie lived on the edge of campus for her son's college years, then built a Foursquare in the Heights, which certainly expressed her own taste and expectations.

A more complicated case is the Cullom-Butler family, who built a late-Victorian cottage on Colcord. Somewhat like multigenerational African American families, getting by was an all-hands-on-deck affair: this was a white working-class family. Cornelius Cullom was a bill collector, and his wife, Rassalee, was secretary to the Waco superintendent of public schools. Their daughter, Marian, and her husband, Thomas Butler, were teachers; and after Thomas died, Marian moved in with her parents and got a job teaching at the new Waco High School, a job she held for decades. And like African American families such as Sam and Hettie Johnson (see *Historic Homes*, 23) they were of limited financial means but great believers in education: Marian's son, Thomas Cullom Butler, earned his PhD in pharmacology and taught for many years at the University of North Carolina.

A final Waco woman discussed in this book is Julia May Sarratt, known after her marriage as Julia Sarratt Sinclair. She was a homeopathic physician, and after moving to Waco around 1905, she practiced in the Provident Building, then the most impressive commercial structure in Waco. Beyond her professional life she was a leader at her church, St. Paul's Episcopal, and belonged to the Business and Professional Women's Club and the Shakespeare Club. Though Julia's career was somewhat avant-garde, the house of John and Julia on Colcord was a fairly conventional expression of the late-Victorian style.

———•———

Most of the houses in this book have not had an architect identified. I do not see this as a problem because many represent what is essentially a builder's vernacular or, to be a bit more precise, a contractor's vernacular. That being said, I have identified the architect for another fourteen houses. Birch Easterwood, who designed twenty of the houses in *Historic Homes*, can take credit for an additional six in *More Historic Homes*. In *Historic Buildings* we have seen that Easterwood also designed churches, skyscrapers, commercial buildings, a middle school, and many buildings at Baylor University. He played an important role in creating the look of Waco.

No new Milton W. Scott houses have been identified, but two houses can now be attributed to architects who once worked in his office. E. McIver Ross, who designed the house of Judge James Alexander on Oriental Road (see *Historic Homes*, 89), also designed the house of C. S. and Regina Appell. Herman F. Cason, who was a draftsman for Scott and a sometime partner of Ross, designed three houses in this book in addition to three in *Historic Homes*. Together with his designs for St. John's Methodist Church facing Seley Park and the Elite Café (now known as Magnolia Table) Cason is clearly a Waco architect who deserves to be better known. In this book we also learn that the house of Harvey Mac Richey can now be credited to Roy E. Lane. It is one of the Waco houses most in tune with the Prairie school of Frank Lloyd Wright and his Chicago compatriots.

There were but a handful of out-of-town architects identified in *Historic Homes*, but they designed some prominent houses: the Rotan-Dossett house by Thomas B. Annan of St. Louis and the Mrs. William Barron house by Bertram C. Hill of Dallas. Although many commercial buildings, churches, and some college buildings were designed by out-of-towners, I have uncovered only two more houses. One of them is by Wilford S. Bogue, a young Fort Worth architect for whom I can find no other houses and very few buildings at all. The other is the Dallas firm of DeWitt and Swank. DeWitt had been involved in the design of high schools in Dallas, buildings at Southern Methodist University, and the Dallas Museum of Fine Arts at Fair Park and served as one of the "Monuments Men" during World War II, tracking down art that had been stolen by the Nazis; Swank had worked with O'Neil Ford on such major designs as the Little Chapel in the Woods at Texas Women's University in Denton.

The surviving houses of Waco form an intricate tapestry, with materials contributed by black Wacoans as well as white; by immigrants from abroad and by people born elsewhere in the United States, as well native Texans; and by homeowners and renters, rich and poor. These houses tell stories of successes and failures, triumphs and tragedies, dreams that came true and dreams that were denied. These houses speak to the complexity of the human condition and to the ongoing experiments that are the city of Waco, the state of Texas, and the United States of America.

Victorian Homes

121. Meredith and Annie Sullivan House

610 N. Sixteenth Street / 1887–88

This Victorian cottage is an amazing survivor. Dating to the 1880s, it was home to two generations of the Sullivan family. Like many a Victorian house it has projecting bays on three sides, complicated hipped roofs, multiple gables, and a dormer window that angles back underneath its dormer. And like most Victorian houses in Waco it had a wrap-around porch, but this one feature was handled differently. In most Waco houses on a corner lot, the porch faces the main street and wraps around to also face the side street; this maximizes the see-and-be-seen nature of the porch. Here the porch wraps around to the south side rather than faces Barron. It may well be that the porch was oriented in that direction because it faced town and that there was very little beyond Barron to look at. Southeast was the direction from which company—or even passersby—would be coming.

Both Meredith A. Sullivan and Annie Ola Burnham were in Waco by the time of the 1880 US Census. In that year he was 27 and she was 18. Meredith was from Massachusetts, and Annie from Tennessee. They married in 1882, and their only son, Richard, came along in 1885. By 1884 Meredith was the teller at the Waco State Bank on Franklin; he soon rose to assistant cashier, then cashier, a position he held for many decades. In addition to his work as a banker, from 1886 to 1899 Meredith was the secretary-treasurer of the Burnham Land, Livestock and Farming Company. The president of this company was Richard E. Burnham, his father-in-law, and the vice president was Richard O. Burnham, his brother-in-law. By 1923 he was also the vice president of the Waco Drug Company. One of Annie's sisters married J. W. Riggins, a future mayor of Waco and the developer of the Riggins (later Raleigh) Hotel (see *Historic Buildings*, 56). Meredith was remembered as a tall man with a long white beard; Annie was remembered for her social work and service to the community.

Son Richard did not seem to inherit the business gene from his father. He stayed in school only through the eighth grade. In 1904 he was a charter member of a Waco glee club known as the Forty Singers. Their formal debut occurred in November 1906 at the old Auditorium Building at Columbus Avenue and North Sixth. In the program for that event Richard was given the nickname "A Foot-light Star." He continued to live at home and did not seem to fall into a regular occupation. For a while he tried work as a traveling salesman. He is said to have served his country in World War I. However, 67-year-old Meredith told the census taker in 1920 that the 34-year-old Richard's occupation was "sport."

Annie Sullivan died in 1922, and Meredith in 1927. As the only child, Richard inherited the house and also a ranch out on Hog Creek northwest of town. He did not work on the ranch himself but hired someone else to manage it. In 1928 he married Fay Hoffman, who was a dancer and taught dancing with her sister Babe. In fact, Fay, Babe, and their older brother Harry were all members of the Forty Singers, although it is not clear when they joined or how long they were members. Fay moved from her parents' house at 1813 Webster, also built around 1888, into this one. (That house was later moved to 810 S. Fourth Street; see *Historic Homes*, 11.) In 1928 Richard gave his occupation as cameraman, although it is unclear if this was his profession or preoccupation. In the 1930 census Richard gave his occupation as farmer. Richard was 45, and Fay was 33. Also living in the household was Tillie Clay, a 46-year-old African American who worked as their cook.

The marriage was over by 1932. Fay got the house in the settlement and promptly sold it. She moved back to 1813 Webster, and Richard moved into the State House Hotel. Neither remarried. In 1940 he seems to have been living on the ranch and identified himself as a farmer. In his later years Richard traveled the world and spent his winters in Florida. When he was in Waco, he would settle into a hotel. When he died in 1956, he was living in the Raleigh Hotel, which had been built for his uncle, J. W. Riggins, between 1912 and 1914. His obituary in the *Waco News-Tribune* remembered him as a "tall, leisurely, long-smiling Wacoan." ■

122. Fred and Marie Koos House

1507 Clay Avenue / 1888

This is one of the oldest houses in this neighborhood and one of the oldest in Waco. It was built for a pair of immigrants: Frederick Koos was a native of Baden-Württemberg in Germany, and Marie Gloor was born in Aargau, Switzerland. They met and married in Waco and started a family. Of the six children, four lived into adulthood: Roy, Fred Oscar, Ida, and Helen. Soon after coming to Waco in the mid-1880s, Fred got a job with the Tom Padgitt Company as a harness maker, and he worked there for decades. When the census taker came by in 1900, Fred gave his occupation as saddler; in 1920 he gave the broader occupation of leather worker. The Koos family belonged to the German Evangelical Zion's Church, which was nearby at 629 S. Eighth (see *Historic Buildings*, 4). Fred died in 1940 at age 85; Marie continued to live in this

122. Fred and Marie
Koos House

house until her death in 1954. Her obituary noted that she had been living in the house for sixty-six years.

The house was one of four frame houses on the north side of the street, only two of which survive. Next door at 1513 Clay were John T. Tyler and his family; he was a drummer (that is, a traveling salesman) and later an insurance agent. At 1517 Clay was a smaller house, briefly occupied by Henry Lazenby, a son of Robert Lazenby, president of the Artesian Manufacturing and Bottling Co. (see *Historic Homes*, 32; and *Historic Buildings*, 43), who worked for his father as a shipping clerk, then foreman, then superintendent; he may have built the present house at 1517 Clay circa 1903. For a few years Samuel P. Herbert, the Waco architect and sometime partner of W. W. Larmour, lived with his wife, Lena, at the other end of the block at 1525 Clay. The house at 1507 Clay is a well-designed example of a Victorian house; perhaps Herbert designed it for his neighbor. ■

123. Charles and Maude Hamilton House

1521 Austin Avenue   /   Circa 1891–92, enlarged by 1926, remodeled 1950s

This rambling one-story Victorian has gone through many changes over the years. Built in the early 1890s, it originally had a wooden frame covered with clapboards and at some later date received a veneer of limestone, which makes it unlike any other Victorian house in Waco. Originally the house was a typical one-story of its time, albeit with a large footprint. The parlor projected forward on the left, and the porch was attached to this and wrapped around on the right side, which was the side facing downtown.

Sometime between 1899 and 1926 the house was improved with a larger front porch, a new porte cochere on the right, and a garage on the alley. The porch now ran all the way across the front, about four feet deep on the left side and about twelve feet deep in the middle and on the right side. The house was still entirely of wood. The garage was one and a half stories and presumably had an apartment.

The original occupants of the house were Otis W. David; his wife, Isla (Lawson) David; and his widowed mother, Eliza P. David. Otis was a native of Georgia, and Isla was from Alabama. Otis worked as the state and county tax collector and therefore had an office in the old county courthouse at Second and Franklin. The year he and Isla built this house Otis opened a livery and carriage stable on the north side of the public square. Apparently the construction of this

123. Charles and Maude Hamilton House

house was the high point of their marriage. By 1900 they were not living together; Isla was living with her younger sister, Marian, and her son. Isla died in 1902. In 1910 Otis was working as an accountant and living in an East Waco boarding house; he died that same year.

Charles and Maude Hamilton purchased the house in 1893. Charles was a native of Meadville, Pennsylvania, and Maude of Mansfield, Ohio. Maude never knew her father, John Wise, because he was killed in 1852 while driving to a presidential campaign rally for Franklin Pierce in a wagon full of explosives that blew up. (John was a member of the Mansfield Gun Squad, and apparently they had been planning a really big twenty-one-gun salute.) In the Civil War Charles fought on the Union side.

Charles and Maude married in 1872 in Rock Island, Illinois. They came to Waco in 1890, where Charles worked with the Texas Central Railroad, serving as vice president and general manager. Charles retired around 1912, but he kept a private office, first in the Amicable Life Insurance Company (ALICO) building and later in the Bankers Trust Building. Also living with them was Maude's mother, Sarah A. Wise. The Hamiltons belonged to St. Paul's Episcopal Church (see *Historic Buildings*, 1). Charles was a member of the vestry—that is, the lay leadership of the church.

The Hamiltons usually had two live-in servants, a cook and a coachman or yard man, usually African American. In 1894 a black man named Harry Reid was living behind their house; he was a porter at the Texas Central Railroad, where Charles was vice president. In 1898 Franklin C. Carter lived out back and worked as a janitor at the railroad offices. According to W. E. B. Du Bois, Colonel Hamilton had been outspoken in his disgust at the lynching of Jesse Washington, "but said that if he led in a protest they would do the same thing to him." Such was the power of intimidation in the Jim Crow South. After the lynching when Hamilton registered at a hotel, he would not indicate that he was from Waco.

Charles died in 1927. Maude continued to live in the house (her mother had died in 1921) but took in a boarder and cut back to one servant (her cook, Hallie Williams) to make ends meet. She died in 1936. Because she and Charles had no children, she made a substantial donation to St. Paul's, and in 1938 a new altar—known as a reredos—was erected in their memory. Maud also willed that their house become a club house for the women of Waco, to be known as Hamilton House. In 1940 the club house had a live-in hostess, Evelyn Bain, and a live-in butler, Emmett Bell. The club remained in operation into the twenty-first century but more recently was converted first into an antique shop and then into law offices.

Sometime in the 1950s the house was recovered with a trendy limestone veneer. At first the veneer covered simply the piers and balustrade of the front porch, but later the walls of the house were also veneered; at this time the right side of the front porch was enclosed to create another room, and the door from the porte cochere was replaced with a window. The phase-2 veneer stone was of a darker color and not as heavily rusticated as the limestone of the piers—perhaps the phase-2 material was some type of artificial stone. In recent decades, all three chimneys have been removed from the house. ◼

    Chapter One

124. Patrick and Nora Cahill House

618 S. Twelfth Street   /   Circa 1891–92

This little house was built for an Anglo-Irish immigrant saloon keeper and was later home to a variety of working-class African Americans. Patrick T. Cahill was born in England to Irish parents. His family immigrated to the United States in 1863, when he was but an infant. Pat married Nora McCarthy around 1887; her family had emigrated directly from Ireland when she was 17. Pat and Nora came to Waco around 1888 and worshipped at St. Mary's Catholic Church, then the only Catholic church in town. At first Pat was a bartender at Alexander Campbell's Waco Saloon, but by 1892 he was running his own saloon at South Eighth and Franklin. As part of being a saloon keeper Pat was an agent for one brewery or another: first for Magnolia Brewing Company of Houston from 1896 to 1900 and later for Pabst Brewery of Milwaukee. Pat and Nora had one daughter, Nellie, who was born in 1892, just as her parents were settling into this house.

When the Cahills lived here, the house had a front porch, two fairly large front rooms separated by a central passage, and a back room on the left side. The house had a wood frame, and its roof was covered with wooden shingles. Originally there were two chimneys; one was on the

124. Patrick and Nora Cahill House

outer side wall of the south room, and the other was on the wall between the front and back rooms on the north side. Sometime before 1899 two small rooms were added immediately behind the central passage; these were the first rooms to have a metal roof. (One of those was probably the first indoor bathroom on the property.) And by 1926 another room was added behind the original back room. The Cahills probably were responsible for none of these additions as around 1896 they moved two blocks to 618 S. Tenth, a one-story Victorian house a few doors down from the Schneider-Pinto house (see *Historic Homes*, 20).

In 1900 the house on Twelfth was occupied by Harris Woods, an African American businessman, and his five children. Harris was a native of Mississippi, but all of his children were born in Texas. Gustavia, who went by Gussie, was 18, Andrew was 15, Harriet was 10, Jessie was 8, and Mattie was 4. Harris Woods seems to have left town soon after the census was taken, but his two oldest children stayed. Andrew got a job working for Madison Cooper, at that time living in a one-story Victorian house at 915 Washington and contemplating building something more impressive on Austin Avenue. Andrew probably worked as the family's coachman and lived in a room attached to the stable/garage. For a while Gussie lived in one of a group of small frame houses behind 910 Franklin Avenue, but in 1902 she was back in this house.

By the time of the 1910 census the house was once again occupied by a white person, James M. McCorkile. Like the Woods family, however, he was working class. He worked for a while as an oiler for the Geyser Ice Company on Jackson and then as a fireman for the Brazos Packing Company. Again, his stay was short, as in 1911 an African American couple, Abraham B. Jackson and his wife, Annie, occupied the house. In 1911 Abe was working as the gardener for Flora Cameron, the widow of William Cameron. There was definitely enough work for a gardener since the Cameron house at 1223 Austin occupied more than two-thirds of the block, and at least half of that was given over to the garden. The physical distance to 618 S. Twelfth was little more than half a mile, meaning it would be an easy walk for Abe, but the social distance between this small cottage and the Victorian mansion was immense. In 1913 Abe had a new job as janitor at the First Baptist Church. The recently completed church by Allen and Scott at North Fifth and Webster was also a half mile from 618 (see *Historic Buildings*, 2).

By 1917 Abe had moved on to another job and another home, and this house was now occupied and apparently owned by a single African American woman, Ella Walker. (She was listed as the owner in the 1917–18 and 1923–24 city directories.) Born in Tennessee around 1875, Ella was the longtime cook of Thomas and Mary Bush, who lived at 1421 Austin Avenue (see 143 in this book). Again, this was a pretty easy walk, though the Bushes seem to have had rooms for servants available as well. Ella also rented out some of her house to other African Americans. In 1919 she rented to Thomas H. Hill and his wife, Frances. Thomas was the owner/operator of the Serve U Garage at 122 Franklin, which was in the black business district just off the town square. The garage serviced automobiles but also did "expert repair work of all kinds." In 1921 she rented to Earl and Ozella Jones. Earl was a washman at the Waco Steam Laundry at the northeast corner of Second and Franklin in the old county courthouse, which had recently been abandoned with the completion of the new courthouse on Washington.

Ella's little house was across the street from the much larger two-story house of Dr. George Conner (see *Historic Homes*, 51), but it is striking that an African American woman in the 1910s and 1920s could achieve the American dream of owning her own home. ■

    Chapter One

125. Richard and Mary Munroe House

2417 Ethel Avenue   /   1893, circa 1914

This house was most likely among the first group of houses built in the Provident Heights Addition by Samuel Colcord, though its age is somewhat obscured by a remodeling circa 1914.

In March 1893 the *Waco Morning News* reported that Dr. Samuel Colcord of New York had bought one-half of the Provident Addition for $70,000. A little over a week later he announced that he was ready to start immediately on the construction of six houses. The Munroe house may be one of those first four or may have been started shortly thereafter. Dr. Colcord seems to have turned to Waco leading architect W. W. Larmour. The last page of Larmour's *Architectural Waco* showed drawings for four two-story residences destined for the Provident Addition. Unlike most of the houses in this booklet, none of them have the name of an owner, suggesting they were designed as part of a real estate speculation. Of the houses in *Architectural Waco*, forty-two were two story and only eight were one story, but clearly Larmour was willing to design houses large or small.

125. Richard and Mary Munroe House

Richard Irby Munroe and Mary Lelia (Davidson) Munroe, usually known as Mamie, were both natives of Quincy, Florida. Richard's father was from Inverness, Scotland, and his mother from Virginia. Mary's father was from Florida, and her mother from Virginia. Richard traveled to Atlanta to attend Emory College (now University). He graduated in 1878 and was admitted to the bar the next year. Richard was in Waco by 1882, establishing his law practice. Richard and Mamie had known each other since childhood, and they married in 1883. In the mid-1880s Munroe partnered with Richard Henry Harrison, who was only one year older than Munroe but with deep Waco roots. Both his father, James E. Harrison, and his uncle Thomas Harrison had been Confederate generals; his aunt Eliza Harrison Earle was the original owner of the Earle-Harrison house (see *Historic Homes*, 3), and his uncle Thomas a later owner.

Munroe served as city attorney for several years around 1890, but for many years he was in private practice, with his office in the Provident Building, the great commercial building at Franklin and Fourth. In 1908 he was appointed judge of the 54th Judicial District Court, which meant moving his office to the second floor of the new McLennan County Courthouse (see *Historic Buildings*, 65). He was later elected to the position and then reelected many times. Richard and Mamie's first son, Richard Jr., was born and died in 1884. Their second son, William Robert Munroe, was born in 1886 and attended Baylor before receiving an appointment to the US Naval Academy in 1904; he went on to a long career in in the navy, rising to the rank of vice admiral.

A historic photograph shows that as built in 1893 the house demonstrated typical Victorian irregularity. A prominent gable above a bay window on the right side projected forward the same distance as the bay; brackets at both corners made the transition from the main wall to the gable. To the left was the front porch, with slim, turned columns along with more Victorian trim. Inside, the parlor was on the right, with its fireplace on the side wall. Later a French door was installed, opening onto the side porch. Behind the parlor were the dining room, pantry, and kitchen; bedrooms were on the west side. Most door and window frames inside had bull's-eye corner blocks. (A house at 902 N. Tenth retains front windows and gable decoration that is extremely close to the original decoration on the Munroe house.)

Around 1914 Richard and Mary Munroe remodeled the house, making it an updated version of the Queen Anne style, which in Texas meant incorporating some classical elements. The porch was enlarged and given squat Ionic columns resting on brick piers; these were just forward of the front and west side walls. At the same time a new porch with matching columns was added on the east side and more rooms on the west, and the hipped roof was expanded accordingly. Judge Munroe was certainly aware of the new taste for all things neoclassical, as he had his office in the McLennan County Courthouse, designed by J. Riely Gordon. A new front door with side lights was installed, providing more light to the entry, and inside, the windows were given new classical surrounds. All these improvements led to an increased valuation for property taxes in 1915.

After their son left for Annapolis in 1904, this house was essentially an empty nest. For some six years, from around 1906 to 1912, they had a live-in servant, Estelle (or Estella) Green, who was 27, African American, and divorced; she worked as the family's cook. In 1910 she was recorded as white in the US Census, but all city directories in which she appeared noted that she was "colored."

A biographical treatment of Judge Munroe from 1911 described him as being "surrounded by and busy with a farm in embryo of fruit, flowers, and vegetables, where the judge mingles the dignity of his office with that of the American farmer." There is obviously not enough room on the current lot for much farming, but the corner lot where a dentist's office now stands was not built upon during the judge's lifetime and may have served an agricultural purpose.

In 1916 Richard Munroe presided over the trial that concluded with one of the most infamous lynchings in American history, that of Jesse Washington. A woman, Lucy Fryer, was murdered in Robinson, just south of Waco on May 8, and a 17-year-old African American, Jesse Washington, who had worked for the Fryers, was arrested. On the next day the county sheriff took him to Hillsboro and then to Dallas to protect him from angry mobs. A grand jury indicted Washington on May 11, and his trial was held on May 15, lasting about an hour. Judge Monroe struggled to keep order in the courtroom. After four minutes of deliberation, the jury found Washington guilty. Just after the verdict was read, a mob seized Washington and dragged him from the county courthouse to the town square. Apparently Judge Munroe did not attempt to stop them, perhaps fearing for his own life. Washington was lit on fire while still alive, and his body was mutilated. This became known as "the Waco Horror," a long-lasting mark on Waco's reputation but which has often been identified as a turning point in the battle against lynching.

At the time of the 1920 census, Richard and Mamie were the only occupants of the house. Mamie died in 1928 at age 67. Funeral records characterized her cause of death as "general paralysis of the insane." It is unclear whether her mental illness was hereditary or whether it might have been brought on by the horror she and her husband had witnessed in May 1916. In 1930 the judge was a widower, and the only other members of the household were two African Americans who worked as servants, Sarah Washington, 33, and Clara N. Washington, 17. By this time a small separate dwelling had been built in the backyard. In 1940 the judge, now retired, was still living in the main house by himself; living out back was an African American man, R. J. Howard, 52 and divorced, who paid five dollars rent each month. The judge died in February 1942 at age 83. ◼

126. Joseph and Adeline Perry House

519 N. Thirteenth Street / 1895

This is a good example of a Victorian house for a middle-class family. It was frame and only one story, but the roof was steeply hipped. The dormer windows on the front and side suggest that space in the attic was utilized. The projection on the south side indicated the placement of the dining room, with the kitchen behind. Two frame outbuildings were at the back of the lot. The house was valued at $4,000 in 1930, a far cry from newer and large houses that were valued at $25,000 or more.

The house was built around 1895 for Joseph and Adeline Perry. Joseph was a native of Maryland, and Adeline (née Sigler) was born in Virginia. They came to Texas after the Civil War. Joseph was a real estate agent (apparently collecting rent much of the time), but both of his sons found work with the railroad. William L. Perry was a railroad station agent at Morgan in Bosque County, then a traveling auditor for the Texas Central Railroad and then for the Missouri, Kansas and Texas Railroad, known as the "Katy." (For the house of his boss at Texas Central, see 123 in this book.) Hugh H. Perry was a railroad shipping clerk; in 1900 he and his wife, Alice, were also living in this house. The family took in boarders to make ends meet. Although a Presbyterian church was built across the street from the house at the same time, the Perry family were Baptist and attended Columbus Street (now Avenue) Baptist Church, which was close by.

Joseph Perry died in 1908. His funeral was at the new church at 1300 Columbus, and he was buried at Oakwood Cemetery. By the time of the 1910 census, Adeline was 71; and her older son, William, had moved into the house, along with his wife, Lilla, and their two daughters, Irene and Louise. They still took in boarders, widows Mary Cheatham and Mattie Rufus. Adeline died in 1912.

In 1920 William and Lilla were still living there, along with daughter Louise, 18, and a student. William died in 1921, and Lilla lived there until her death in 1941. In 1930 she was joined by her daughter, Irene Oden, who was a widow at 31. Irene's husband, Irwin A. Oden, had been the chief clerk to the auditor of the MKT railroad in Dallas, and after his death, Irene moved home and worked for several years as a stenographer for the MKT. Ten years later Lilla, age 74, was renting to two boarders and gave her occupation as bookkeeper of a missionary society.

By 1926 there were eight houses on this side of the street, plus another two facing Jefferson Avenue. In 1950 the two houses closest to Barron had been demolished for Waco Drive, the artery created to allow commuters to rapidly retreat to the suburbs. ■

126. Joseph and Adeline Perry House

127. Hardie H. and Bessie M. Holt House

524 Dallas Street   /   Circa 1896

The original owners of this house were Hardie H. and Bessie M. Holt. Hardie (sometimes spelled Hardy) was a passenger conductor for the Texas Central Railroad. (For the house of his boss at Texas Central, see 123 in this book.) This was a logical neighborhood in which to live because the passenger depot was on Elm Avenue. Hardie and Bessie were married around 1892 and moved into this house by 1896. They owned the house free and clear by 1900. By 1910 they could afford a live-in cook.

The one-story house is in the early version of the Queen Anne style with ornamental brackets and thin, turned posts rather than stout classical columns as on the Pippin House at 502 Dallas. The roof is steep and complicated, echoing the complicated floor plan beneath. Many changes have been made over the years. The front door was replaced with a large window, a single piece of plate glass; one of two tall windows on the left front room has been converted into a door; and there is a door, possibly original, into the right front room. These are signs that the house was subdivided into two or three units at some time in its history. And the back porch of the south (left) side was enclosed to create another room.

After some twenty-five years in the house, Hardie and Bessie moved across the river to 2201 Austin Avenue. Hardie continued to work as a conductor, and the Holts rented out the house on Dallas. Around 1919–20, Hardie tried his hand at opening an automobile supply store and repair shop. This enterprise was not successful, as he was back to being a conductor by 1923. However, Hardie and Bessie divorced, and in 1928 Bessie moved back into 524 Dallas. To generate some income, she took in boarders, starting with Thomas Yarbrough, who worked as a janitor, and his wife, May. By 1930 Hardie had remarried and was living at 110 S. Twenty-Fourth Street. He passed away around 1936 or 1937; in 1938 Bessie was still living at 524 Dallas and listed as a widow. ◼

127. Hardie H. and Bessie M. Holt House

128. Edward and Elizabeth Jones House
(Jones-Carothers-Rowell House)

1601 Columbus Avenue   /   Circa 1897, remodeled circa 1920

This house was built for a prominent Waco attorney, his second wife, and his children from both marriages. It was later owned by the manager of a company that made doors and window sashes and then by the owner of a furniture store. It started out as a fairly typical Waco version of the Queen Anne style: two stories, frame, with a garage out back. The prominent, nearly triangular gables spoke to the popularity of the Queen Anne style, as did the porch, which wrapped around to face Sixteenth Street and downtown.

The original occupants were Edward A. Jones; his wife, Elizabeth; and six children. Edward was a native of Maryland, a Confederate veteran (the 28th Mississippi Cavalry), and an attorney. He was partner in the law firm of Jones & Sleeper, along with William Markham Sleeper, who was a longtime judge and chair of the Waco Water Commission. His first wife was Lucy Markham Jones, a native of Mississippi, whose sister Martha was married to William M. Sleeper. Lucy died in Waco in 1884, and in 1889 Edward married Elizabeth Steel Latta Spann. In addition to several children by Lucy, Edward had one child with Lizzie. In 1898 the Jones family had one live-in servant, Emily Wehring; her sisters Louise and Lydia were also in service to prominent Waco families. Their parents, Henry and Mina Wehring, had emigrated from Germany to Texas and farmed first in Washington County near Brenham, where their daughters were born, and later in Falls County.

In 1900 Edward's oldest daughter, Bessie, 37, was married to Roy G. Patton, a native of Pennsylvania and a real estate agent; they lived next door at 1906 Columbus. Roy and Bessie had three young children: Robert, Edward, and Elizabeth. Also living with them were two servants: Hannah Foster, a Norwegian-born 35-year-old widow, and Clarence Jackson, a 30-year-old black Texas native. Clarence was born a free man, but it is highly likely that both his parents, also native Texans, had been enslaved. (Edward's oldest son, George W. Jones, 31, was living at home but working as a bookkeeper for his brother-in-law.) The Patton house was another frame Queen Anne, which has since been demolished.

Tragedy struck the family when Edward A. Jones died in September 1900 at age 54. The funeral was at St. Paul's Episcopal Church (see *Historic Buildings*, 1), and the burial at Oakwood Cemetery. Lizzie was now widowed for a second time at age 45. She and the children continued to live at 1601 Columbus for several years—like many widows, Lizzie took in a boarder or two, such as Sidney T. Maxwell, an insurance agent. The Jones family had moved on by 1906, when the house was occupied by Richard B. King, the general manager of the American Freehold Land Mortgage Company, which had its offices in the Provident Building at Franklin and Fourth.

A year later the occupants were Samuel and Lollie Carothers, both natives of Illinois. Samuel was the manager of the Waco Sash & Door Company, while Lollie ran the household. In 1910 two of their five children were living with them: John, 27, and William, 21. John was a traveling salesman, and William was an auto salesman; they were born in Missouri and Kansas, respectively, an indication of some of the places the family had lived before coming to Texas. The family stayed in this house about five years before buying a small Victorian house at 1819 Washington,

next door to the Duffield-Whitworth house. The house at 1819 was older and smaller than this one, but the Carothers family could now afford two live-in servants.

The house at 1601 Columbus was vacant in 1916, but the next year Hugh and Eleanor Williams rented it. They were new to Waco, but Hugh was making a splash by opening the Williams Dry Goods Company, which dealt in dry goods wholesale, and by erecting a building at 216 S. Sixth Street (1917–18; see *Historic Buildings*, 50). The Williams family included two daughters and a son, all under the age of 10, and Hugh's widowed mother, Maria, who was 76 in 1920. They could also afford a cook, Freda Hander, who was a native of Texas born of German parents. Hugh had come to town with the financial backing of the Mercantile Trust Company of St. Louis, but he apparently did not get along with his local investors, and after he was eased out of the position of president in 1922, the name was changed to the Waco Dry Goods Company. In 1921 the Williams family had moved to a house at 224 N. Eighth Street, and they left Waco within a year or so.

128. Edward and Elizabeth Jones House (Jones-Carothers-Rowell House)

Around 1920 Ray and Byrde Rowell purchased and remodeled the house at 1601 Columbus. The original turned columns were replaced with brick piers that were more closely aligned

with the style of bungalows and other manifestations of the arts and crafts movement. A matching porte cochere was also added on the Sixteenth Street side. Originally the house had a one-and-a-half-story frame barn at the northeast corner, abutting Sixteenth Street. Presumably the half story included quarters for their male servant, Clarence Jackson. By 1926 this barn was gone, replaced by a frame one-story garage at the northwest corner of the lot, which had exposed rafter ends in a style typical of bungalows.

Ray owned the Waco Furniture Company at 205–207 Washington and also the East Side Furniture Company at 516–518 Elm. He and Byrde had one son and one daughter and in 1920 could afford to have a live-in African American cook, Mary Ella Murry. ◼

129. James N. and Sarah Harris House

1216 Dallas Street   /   Circa 1899

This was the third Waco house of James and Sarah Harris, and their largest. James N. Harris was a native of Calhoun County, Alabama, who became a brick manufacturer and contractor—sometimes in conjunction with Sion (a.k.a. Simon) Trice. Sarah Kennedy Harris came to Texas from Giles County, Tennessee. They first lived on South Third Street in a two-story brick house built in 1879; James sold it to William Davis in 1885. (It was demolished in the 1960s for the construction of Interstate 35.) He then built a house at 1316 Washington Avenue, which was a simple brick house with an ornate Victorian porch. Inside was a central passage with a room to each side and a kitchen behind the left front room (see *Historic Homes*, 9).

129. James N. and Sarah Harris House

As 1900 approached, James N. Harris was 60 years old, and his son Frank had become a partner in the brickyard, by then known as J. N. Harris & Son. James and Sarah decided to move to East Waco to be closer to the brickyard. They sold the house on Washington to James H. Sturgis and moved into this house. In 1900 the household included James and Sarah; older son, Harvey; younger son, Frank, and his wife, Minnie, and their three children. Also living there were two African American servants, Theodore and Martha Ashley. However, the city directories make clear that Theodore Ashley was actually the foreman at the brickyard. By 1910 the Ashleys had moved on; Susal Washington, a 68-year-old African American, was working as the family's cook.

Strikingly, this was the first frame house for James and Sarah, though it rests on a tall brick base, doubtless from the Harris brickyard. While many Victorian houses had a porch that wrapped around one side, the Harris house had a porch only on the front, though the roof was supported by ornate turned columns and gingerbread brackets. The chimney, which looks to be early if not original, rises in the center of the roof, and fireplaces heat three rooms below. The entrance leads into a heated stair hall; the stair is at the back of the space. To the left was the parlor, and behind this was the dining room. The kitchen was originally at the back right but in a recent rehabilitation has been moved to the space behind the dining room. As of 1926 there were four small outbuildings in the backyard, one of them brick. The house originally had a shingled roof, including the roof of the porch. ■

130. Victorian Single-Wall Rent House

716 Pecan Avenue   /   Circa 1899

This is late-Victorian working-class housing at its most basic: four rooms and a roof over your head. Moreover, the walls that kept out the wind and rain and—very occasionally—snow were a single layer. That is to say, the framing was kept to an absolute minimum. One layer of boards, arranged vertically, were given some sort of stability by corner posts and by the clapboards that were nailed to the external side of those boards. Thus, there were no internal walls that might allow insulation to be placed in between the inner and outer walls. So thin were the walls that each window, flush with the outer walls, projected into the rooms!

130. Victorian Single-Wall Rent House

The house had a typical Victorian irregular floor plan, specifically a T plan; that is, there are three rooms lined up on the right side and a wing roughly in the middle on the left. The function of the four rooms is not entirely clear, but it seems likely that there were a living room, a kitchen, and perhaps two bedrooms. There was not an indoor bathroom—such a space was becoming typical in well-to-do houses but was still out of reach for the working class. There were, however, front and back porches, which allowed some hope of cool spaces to sit during sultry Waco evenings.

Originally the house was numbered as 608 Pecan; between 1907 and 1910 it was renumbered as 716, which it remains today. The earlier known occupants were the Mullins family, who were recorded in the 1900 US Census. Benjamin, a native of Tennessee, was something of a jack of all trades: between 1898 and 1902 he was noted as a laborer, a watchman, and a carpenter. His wife, Marge, was a native of Texas, but both of her parents had been born in England. They were living with their three daughters, Emma, Tressa, and Lena, and with Marge's younger sister, Gertrude. Apparently the family left Waco shortly after 1902.

By 1906 the house was home to a widow, Mignon B. Williford, and her children. In the 1890s she and her husband, James Williford, had been living in northern Bosque County. Both James and Mignon were natives of Tennessee. However, James died in 1895, leaving her with three small children and another on the way. Sometime between 1900 and 1906 she decided to move her growing family into Waco. In 1910 the occupants of this house were Mignonette, 44; Carl, 22; Sallie, 19; Margaret, 16; and James, 13. None of the children had an occupation yet, and Mignonette reported that she was living off her own income, which suggests either that James had left her well-off or that she had brought substantial resources to the marriage. A year later Carl was working as a mechanical engineer, James as a clerk, and both girls as seamstresses.

The family had moved on by 1913, and by 1916 the residents were Samuel E. Fowler and his family. In 1920 Samuel, a native of South Carolina, was 61 and working as a teamster for the Pierce Fordyce Oil Company. His wife Cornelia, 59, was working at home, while daughter Yula Bell, 16, was still in school. Their son Orell, 30, was working as a laborer at the Exporters & Traders Compress & Warehouse Company, known today as Extraco, which compressed and stored cotton from the farms of McLennan and surrounding counties. Though they were not wealthy, Samuel and Cornelia owned their little house. The longest-term early owners were Ed and Alice Thomason; Ed was from Kentucky, while Alice was a Texas native. Ed was a laborer at the nearby Extraco warehouse. By 1930 Ed was 60, widowed, and working at the compress, but still living in this house. He was joined by his son Joe, 30, and Joe's wife, Mary, 31. The little house was valued at $1,200, though ten years later, in the midst of the Great Depression, Ed estimated that the value had dropped to $500. ◼

131. John L. Pippin House

502 Dallas Street   /   Circa 1906

This house is characteristic of Waco houses—and Texas houses—of the later Queen Anne style. Such houses still had the asymmetry, irregular floor plan, and steeply sloping roof of early Queen Anne houses but also incorporated neoclassical Doric columns on the porch and sedate white walls rather than the earlier Victorian polychromy. It was a one-story house, but the window in the front gable and the large dormer on the south (left) side suggested that there was usable space in the attic.

The house was built for John L. Pippin, who was a horse trader—and a mule trader as well. Though he lived in East Waco, his business was across the river. Pippin would have taken the

Suspension Bridge every day to his lot at 125 Washington. Around 1913 Pippin decided to move across the river to a house at 1915 Franklin. From 1913 to 1921 the house on Dallas was occupied by William D. Wallace, a notary public, and his wife, Kate. (William Jr.; his wife, Sadie; and sister, Verlie, a schoolteacher, lived nearby at 503 Turner.)

The house had a several owners or occupants in the 1920s and 1930s. By 1923 Charles Caswell and his wife, Annie, owned the house. Charles was an engineer for the Houston and Texas Central Railroad. Their occupancy, however, was short. From 1928 to 1934 the occupants were Della Fraser and her adult children, Eldred, Jack, and Mildred. Eldred was an electrician at the Bell Mead Locomotive Shops, and Jack worked with the State Highway Department. In the late 1930s Asa Skinner, a realtor, and his wife, Emma, lived in the house. ◾

132. Wade and Carrie Morrison House (Morrison-Lanham-Crowder House)

1503 Washington Avenue   /   1906

This has been the home of three well-known Wacoans. It was built for Wade B. Morrison, the druggist who suggested that a newly invented soft drink be named Dr Pepper. It was later the home of Dr. Howard M. Lanham, a prominent Waco physician and surgeon. More recently it was the home of Christian rock musician David Crowder. It gained additional fame in 2018 for being placed on the market with a price tag of $1.45 million.

Wade B. Morrison was involved with various partners in a number of businesses associated with drugstores, both wholesale and retail. Over time his retail location was branded the "Old Corner" drug store. In the 1890s he was also the president of the Artesian Manufacturing and Bottling Co. Wade and his wife, Carrie, were 33 and 23, respectively, when they moved into this

132. Wade and Carrie Morrison House (Morrison-Lanham-Crowder House)

house. Their one child, John B. Morrison, was born in 1895. They lived in the house through 1902, but in 1904 they were living in St. Louis, Missouri. When they returned to Waco, they moved into a new house at the southeast corner of Lyle Avenue and Eighteenth Street (now the parking lot for a Dollar General store).

The overall arrangement of the house dates to the Morrisons' tenure. The house was frame, two stories, with a tall hipped roof and gables on three sides. The gable on the Fifteenth Street side retains the most Victorian character, with its shingles and Palladian window. The red, two-story, board-and-batten garage may date from their time as well. Through the 1950s there was a small one-story cottage where the garage now stands. In 1900 Wade and Carrie Morrison had one live-in servant, Bettie Coffee, a 23-year-old African American, and she probably lived in this cottage.

The next owners were Howard and Annie Lanham. Dr. Lanham practiced from a variety of offices: the Provident Building, which was in Waco's grand Victorian business block, as well as two newer rivals, the Praetorian Building and the Amicable Building (now known as the ALICO) (see *Historic Buildings*, 57 and 55). In 1906, when the city directory showed them in this house, they had two daughters, Sarah, 4, and Margaret, 1, and son, Samuel, who was born in that year. Another daughter, Martha, was born in 1910. In the census for that year the family had a live-in nurse, Jeannie Leason, who presumably helped Annie with her four young children. Additionally, an African American couple lived out back: Lee Pugh was the yard man; and his wife, Lyder, was the cook.

The Lanhams updated the house in a number of ways. The front porch with its neoclassical Doric columns and solid balustrade dates from their time, as do the neoclassical mantels in some of the rooms. The prominent sleeping porch with casement windows probably dates from their time as well. When this house was built, Fifteenth did not run from Washington to Columbus; there was a one-story frame house next door at 1429 Washington. The house was demolished and the street paved by 1929, when the Gulf filling station was built at 1425 Washington. (This is the reason that the new part of Fifteenth Street is seventy-five feet wide, while the part north of Columbus is only sixty-five feet.)

David and Toni Crowder spent six years restoring the house. David was a Baylor graduate and the leader of the David Crowder*Band. (A photo of the band in the living room was featured on the website for their album *Church Music*.) The two-story, board-and-batten garage was remodeled to contain a recording studio. The house has been subtly enlarged over the years: part of the west side porch has been enclosed, and sometime after 1950 the hipped-roof projection toward Fourteenth Street was added.

The Crowders acquired the empty lot next to the house to create a large side yard where they could have a swimming pool and a gazebo. (Indeed, they installed French doors in the west wall of the dining room to allow for access to the side yard and pool.) When the site was being excavated, workers uncovered construction debris, presumably from 1511 Washington, the two-story house that had stood on the site for many years. The Crowders put it on the market in 2011.

The awnings were added after the Crowder ownership; they were quite popular in Waco in the early twentieth century, an era prior to air conditioning, and several Waco companies made them, notably the Clifton Manufacturing Company ◼

133. John F. and Addie Rowe House

326 N. Fourteenth Street   /   Circa 1906

More late-Victorian houses survive in Waco than most people realize. This one had all the leading characteristics: a tall, hipped roof; a prominent gable in the shape of a nearly equilateral triangle that was filled with shingles; a front room with a bay window; and a porch that wraps around to the side. Both the front gable and a similar one on the south side have paired windows framed with pilasters, both with a bull's eye at the top. The porch was unusual in that it wraps away from the side street of this corner lot. The porch had thin classical columns of the Doric order, where earlier versions of the Queen Anne style would have posts with elaborate turnings. Both of the chimneys seem to be original or at least very early.

For all its Victorian irregularity, the house had a central passage running straight through the house. That hallway had tall wainscoting with plaster walls above, while one of the formal rooms had paneled wainscoting. Windows and doors were framed with moldings and corner blocks, and pocket doors connected two of the public rooms. All of these elements were now available from local lumbers mills, such as Wm. Cameron & Company or its many imitators.

133. John F. and Addie Rowe House

The one-story frame garage on the Barnard Street side looks to be from the same period as the house. The garage door hangs on a pair of Allith fire door hangers made in Chicago, similar to ones on the back door of the Waco Dry Goods Company at 216 S. Sixth Street (see *Historic Buildings*, 50).

This house predates the Shear-Parker-Migel house and the Smith-Callan house by about five years. It was built for John F. Rowe, who was first a traveling accountant and then manager of the credit department at Rotan Grocery. (For the house of the Rotans, go around the corner to 1503 Columbus Avenue, or see *Historic Homes*, 12.) John and his wife, Addie, lived here with his mother, the widow Elizabeth Rowe, who was 72 in 1910, and their son, John Forsythe, who was a student at Baylor University; he eventually became a physician. Also in the household in 1910 were two live-in servants, both African Americans: Oscar Reed, the yard man, and Katie McGhee, the cook. In 1920 John and Addie were still living here, as was Forsythe and his wife, Ethel. Elizabeth Rowe had passed away, and the two servants were no longer with the family. Instead, Bertha Dura was working as their maid. By 1930, however, both generations of the Rowe family had moved to Dallas. ■

134. Pecan Street Shotgun House

715 Peach Avenue (formerly 717)   /   Circa 1906

This extremely simple shotgun house is missing its mate. Originally a second house was just to the right of it, and they were numbered 715 and 717. The two houses were built on one lot, which was typical for shotguns, and they were situated close to the outer edges of the lot, allowing a large common space between them. In fact, both houses had an inset back porch facing

134. Pecan Street Shotgun House

this joint side yard. The surviving one of the pair is the oldest, appearing in the city directory of 1907–08; the other was built sometime between 1913 and 1915 and first appeared in the 1916 city directory. These two wood-frame houses replaced an even smaller wooden house that stood on the lot in 1899.

Shotgun houses had two, three, or four rooms, one behind the other, often with the addition of a front porch. Sometimes the doors between rooms lined up—supposedly a shotgun could be fired through the house without hitting a wall—and other times they did not, but this was not a crucial feature. African roots are often cited for this house type, and precedents certainly

exist there for such houses. However, in Waco, at least, such houses were built as rent houses for anyone, black, white, or brown, who needed cheap lodging. The fact that two such houses could be built on one lot made the building type all the more attractive to potential landlords. Fancier shotgun houses might have a hipped roof—that is, the roof sloped down on all four sides—but this was the basic model, with simple gables front and back.

The original occupants were the members of the Beshear family, and all members labored at low-wage jobs. Thomas Beshear was a wood dealer; Elmer, the oldest son, was a teamster; while Edwin was a laborer; sister Loretta was a toll operator at the Southwest Telephone Exchange; wife and mother, Martha, ran the house. In 1910 Edwin and Elmer were living a few doors down at 711 Pecan with their older sister, Jennetta, and her husband, Henry E. Gorman. Henry was a house carpenter; perhaps he was involved in building houses in this neighborhood. Later Edwin was a city fireman, and Elmer worked at Owens Lumber Company.

Meanwhile, 717 Pecan was the home of Corry and Cordelia Ray and their five children. Corry, a native of Mississippi, was a brick contractor. Their stay was also short, as one year later, in the 1911 city directory, the occupants were a carpenter, S. Edward Fowler, and his family. Fowler later worked as a watchman for the Pierce Fordyce Oil Association, and the family rented several other houses in this neighborhood, including 716 and 725 Pecan. All later occupants here and next door were craftsmen or laborers, except for a minister, the Reverend James A. Blackburn and his wife, Katie. Doubtless all of them dreamed of moving on from housing so basic, but houses like this could keep both them and their dreams alive. ◼

135. Jeremiah and Cordelia Early House

1203 N. Fifth Street   /   Circa 1907

This house may have been built as early as 1907 for Frank Matthews, a ticket agent at Waco's Union Station, but longer-term residents were Jeremiah (Jerry) and Cordelia (Cora) Early, who lived there from 1911 until 1948. Jerry Early was a native of Virginia; Cora Morris was born in Houston. Jerry's older brother, Eugene, was in Waco by 1876, and Jerry himself by 1878. Eugene opened his own grocery in 1880. Cora's father, Joseph R. Morris, was a Connecticut native and the owner of a Houston hardware store; during the Civil War he was a Unionist and during Reconstruction was appointed mayor of Houston. Cora grew up in a house designed and built by Richard Allen, an African American builder who was a talented carpenter before and after freedom came. Jerry and Cora married in 1889, and Jerry settled into a long career as a grocer, selling groceries, produce, wines, and liquors.

The front porch looked quite symmetrical with neoclassical Doric columns and a compatible balustrade. Though there was one front room on the left and an entrance hall, the porch

135. Jeremiah and Cordelia
Early House

wrapped around on the Kentucky Street side, a feature that was a remnant from the Victorian era. The tall hipped roof with multiple gables was also Victorian, though the pediment on the hipped roof of the porch was perfectly centered. The chimneys look to be quite old: original or close to it. The Early family was thoroughly middle class, and there is no evidence that they had servants. They estimated the value of the house as $6,000 at a time when new two-story houses were valued at $20,000 or even $30,000. After ten years of the Great Depression, they valued it at $3,000. ◼

136. Thomas and Emma Sterling House

811 N. Fourth Street / 1907

A substantial African American community grew up north of what is now Waco Drive, centered on North Seventh Street, the original location of New Hope Baptist Church. This house was somewhat on the fringe of this neighborhood but is a good example of how a hardworking multigenerational black family overcame the odds to live in a decent house. Quite unusual for this period is the fact that they owned the house.

Tom Sterling worked a variety of janitorial jobs: at the police station, city hall, a drug store, and a theater. His wife, Emma, was a seamstress, working out of their house. While Emma sewed, their daughter, Martha, kept house. Martha's husband, George Allen, was a porter at Sanger Brothers dry goods store. Martha was also raising their son, Clifford, and daughter, Mabel. In 1920 the family was also bringing in extra income by renting rooms to four boarders.

The tall roof, prominent gables, and asymmetrical floor plan mark this as a late-Victorian house; however, the classical columns on the front porch and the way that the porch ran across the entire front, in spite of the projecting room on the left, indicate that the Sterlings were aware of the rising popularity of the Neoclassical style. By 1926 there was a one-story garage in the back, flanked by a room on each side. These rooms may be where they put two or more boarders. ■

136. Thomas and Emma
Sterling House

137. Sinclair-Sarratt House
(later Good Neighbor Settlement House)

2301 Colcord Avenue / Circa 1911–12

John D. Sinclair was from an old Waco family—which was nevertheless quite thoroughly middle class—while his wife, Julia, was a relatively new arrival and, rare for Waco, a professional woman. John's father, William Sinclair, was the longtime proprietor of a harness and saddle shop on the south side of the Square. The family lived in an older one-story house on South Fifth, just south of the old Baylor University—now the campus of the First Baptist Church. John worked for nearly two decades with the Goldstein-Migel Company, starting as a stock boy, then cashier in the store, but quickly becoming a bookkeeper from around 1892 to 1908.

Julia May Sarratt was born in Steubenville, Ohio, and moved to Waco around 1905. She was an osteopathic physician and had offices in the Provident Building at Fourth and Franklin. She lived for several years at The Kyle, a residential hotel at Twelfth and Franklin. In 1906 Waco had two other osteopaths: one was a male, and the other a married woman. Julia was the first single woman to hang out her shingle; in 1907 she was joined by J. Ellen Gildersleeve, the sister of Fred Gildersleeve, who was just starting his long career as a Waco photographer.

137. Sinclair-Sarratt House (later Good Neighbor Settlement House)

Julia and John married in 1910 or 1911 and soon moved into their new house on Colcord. John ended his long association with Goldstein-Migel and worked in a variety of jobs: secretary of the Retail Merchants Association, secretary-treasurer of the South Bosque Oil Company, as a notary public with an office in the new courthouse, and as an accountant for the August A. Busch Company, which sold a great deal of beer from its headquarters in St. Louis. In 1919 he settled in at the Provident National Bank, first as a teller, then as a bookkeeper and auditor. As a professional woman Julia was unwilling to completely give up her maiden name; she appeared in the city directories as Julia Sarratt Sinclair, Mrs. Julia May Sarratt, Mrs. Julia May Sarratt Sinclair, and Mrs. Julia S. Sinclair.

In 1924 John died suddenly, just short of his fiftieth birthday. Julia continued her homeopathic practice and was also involved in the Business and Professional Women's Club and the Shakespeare Club. A member of St. Paul's Episcopal Church, she worked in the 1930s with the new rector, the Reverend Everett Holland Jones, in planning twelve stained-glass windows that would depict the life of Christ. Julia paid for *The Annunciation* on the north wall, which was in a French style contrasting with the ten Germanic windows by Franz Meyer. The left panel, showing the angel Gabriel, was in memory of John D. Sinclair, while the right panel, depicting the Virgin Mary, was dedicated "To the Glory of God and in Memory of Julia Sarratt-Sinclair." She died in 1937 at age 57.

Apparently, John was willing to have his wife continue her professional career, which suggests a relatively progressive frame of mind, but their house was fairly conservative in style. In fact, it was one of the last Victorian houses in Waco. (It was built when he was 36 and she was 31.) Its Victorian nature is somewhat concealed by the fact that the porch was enclosed by a later owner. The porch stretched across the front and along the side facing Twenty-Third Street, where a door led into the dining room. Presumably the columns were neoclassical, as was usually found on late–Queen Anne houses in Texas. Other Victorian features were the tall, hipped roof (originally covered with shingles of wood, now asbestos) and the shingled gable with semicircular window providing light to the attic space. The trio of windows on the east side had wooden mullions that suggested the Gothic style. Another projection on the west side—the part covered by the main roof—was enlarged to the west before 1950. By 1926 there was a garage at the northeast corner; by 1950 the present two-story apartment was built in front of it. From the early 1940s to the 1990s the house served as a Montessori school known as the Jack & Jill School. In 2010 the house became the Good Neighbor Settlement House, an attempt to foster community in an age when fences are going up to separate neighbors.

The house next door is also early but has been remodeled. The general configuration—two stories, rectangular footprint, hipped roof—is original, but in its earlier appearance there was a one-story porch running across the front. Perhaps that porch was removed when the porte cochere was added on the east side. Originally the drive led back to a garage at the northeast corner. ◼

2316 Colcord Avenue (now 2304) / Circa 1911

This late-Victorian cottage was built for Cornelius Perry Cullom and his wife, who was variously known as Rassalee, Rossalee, or Rosalie. However, it quickly became a three-generational household. The Culloms were a farming family from Middle Tennessee with roots in Kentucky. They had three children, two of whom survived into adulthood. By 1910 they were in Waco, where Cornelius worked as a bill collector and Rassalee worked as a secretary to the superintendent of Waco's public schools. Rassalee had attended college for two years, and her daughter, Marian (a.k.a. Marion), attended for three.

Marian married Thomas B. Butler, a Mississippi native. They briefly lived in Phoenix, Arizona, where Thomas worked as a schoolteacher. Thomas and Marian had a son in Phoenix, Thomas Cullom Butler, born April 2, 1910. When little Thomas was six days old, the US Census taker visited their house, recording that his father was 30 and his mother 26. A few months later the family traveled to Waco—it is unclear whether they were moving there or simply visiting her parents, who were living at 1915 Fort. However, on July 20 Thomas B. Butler died; he was buried in Oakwood Cemetery the next day.

138. Cullom-Butler House

Her parents' new house may have already been under construction when her husband died; by 1911 they were in this house, and Marian and little Thomas were living with them. Marian was able to get a job teaching in the public schools, briefly at one of the elementary schools but by 1913 at the brand-new high school on Columbus Avenue (see *Historic Buildings*, 75). This extended family lived here for more than two decades. In 1930 Cornelius was 81; Rassalee, 67; Marian, 46; and

Thomas, 20. Presumably Thomas left for college soon thereafter; he became a pharmacologist and worked for many years at the University of North Carolina. Cornelius died in 1932, and in 1940 this house was occupied by two widows, Rassalee and Marian, who was still teaching at Waco High. Rassalee died in 1943, and Marian died in 1983, joining Thomas in Oakwood after seventy-three years of widowhood.

This is a case where it is difficult to pick out the original house, because it was greatly expanded sometime after 1950. Their house was one story and frame, with a tall, hipped roof. The front and back porches were both on the west side; these were both enclosed, and a large front porch with a hipped roof was added. (The gable on the left seems to be the only original part of the front wall.) The back of the house was enlarged as well, including a projection to the west. Apparently the bungalow-ish shingled skirt was added when the house was remodeled. Originally there was a long but narrow barn at the southeast corner of the property; by 1950 that had been replaced by a small garage. ■

Bungalows and Foursquares

139. Rogers-Bexley House

2205 Lasker Avenue / Circa 1909

The north side of this block features one example from each of the house styles popular in Waco before World War I. At 2201 is a late-Victorian cottage; at 2205, a side-gabled bungalow; at 2221, a bungalow with two forward-facing gables; and at 2223, a one-story Foursquare with an inset front porch.

There are other examples of side-gabled bungalows in Waco, such as the Lee and Alice Dewey house at 2712 Austin Avenue (see *Historic Homes*, 48) and the Horace and Cora Randle house at 1200 Elm (see *Historic Homes*, 50), but this is the only one to have a jerkin-head roof—that is, the top portions of the gable ends are clipped off. The roof was originally shingled. Unlike some side-gabled bungalows, this one does not have a shed dormer on the roof; in fact, there is no living space in the attic. As in most bungalows, the rafter ends are exposed on the front and back elevations. The roof extends out over the side walls and is supported by brackets. The front porch is set underneath the main roof but does not extend all the way across the front. Windows in pairs and trios abound. There was direct entry into both front rooms. On the west side there was a small inset porch, presumably leading into the kitchen.

Originally this was a rent house, occupied by craftsmen and their families. In 1910 it was occupied by a widow, Tabitha Ann Rogers, and five of her eight children. She was 52 and the widow of John Knox Rogers. Tabitha was a native Texan, but her husband was from Mississippi. In 1910 her oldest boys, John Knox Rogers Jr., 21, and James G. Rogers, 18, were both working as plumbers. Their younger brother, Daniel, 15, was working as a salesman for a wholesale company. The twins, Lucy and Mary, 11, were attending school. The Rogers family moved out within a year.

The new renters were Edward Bexley, 31, and his wife Mamie (Tucker) Bexley, 30. Both were native Texans but with roots in Alabama. Edward characterized his work in various ways over the years—carpenter, cabinetmaker, pattern maker at a planing mill, mechanic—but a specialty of his throughout the years was building stairs. He worked for C. M. Trautschold for a number of years. In 1910 Edward and Mamie had been living with the family of Edgar Woodward, a local real estate developer, so this was their first house. They lived in this house for more than forty years, first as renters but by 1920 as owners. In 1930 they estimated that the house was worth $3,000. Edward died in 1954 while visiting his brother in Aransas Pass; Mamie died in 1960 at age 80. They are buried in Oakwood Cemetery. ■

139. Rogers-Bexley House

140. William and Jennie Colgin House

1902 Austin Avenue   /   1912

The Colgin family had been living on this lot for more than twenty years when they decided to upgrade their house for their retirement years. William E. Colgin was a native of Mobile, Alabama, who came to Waco between 1880 and 1882. He quickly found work at Herman Behrens's drugstore; after a couple of years he switched to the shop of James E. Sears and then opened his own drugstore in 1888. By then he had married Jennie Bailey, a native of St. Louis, Missouri, and had two sons. (A daughter, Monette, and a son, William, would soon round out the family.)

Around 1890 the family had a new address: 1902 Austin Avenue, but were living in an area that Waco had not yet reached. In fact, in 1893 this was part of what was known as "Farm Lot

140. William and Jennie Colgin House

No. 30." It seems highly likely that the Colgin family was in fact farming in this neighborhood. They would not have grown a cash crop but fresh foods to put on their dinner table. It would take a decade or more for other families to join them in the neighborhood.

Probably the decision of the Cooper family to move to Austin and Eighteenth tipped the scales. Soon Sam and Mabel McLendon were building a grand Southern Colonial across the street from the Coopers, and the residential character of the neighborhood was sealed. A key moment came for the Colgin family in February 1912, when they announced that they planned to build a two-story brick residence that would cost some $8,000.

The house was a very compact version of an American Foursquare. The wooden frame had a veneer of demure buff-colored brick. The roof was hipped, with a matching hipped dormer in the middle. The front porch was one story, somewhat enclosed by a low brick wall, upon which rested on Doric piers, either singly or in pairs. A matching porte cochere stretched from the east side wall toward Nineteenth Street. As on many Foursquares there were numerous paired windows.

On a less compact version of a Foursquare, entrance would be into a stair hall that was roughly the same size as the other front room; here it was a narrower side passage on the left side of the

house. The stair was on the outer wall, and it met a stair from the back of the house at the landing and turned to the west to rise to the second floor. Behind the stair was a passage from the porte cochere and then the kitchen. The right side of the first floor held the two principal rooms, the living room and the dining room. There were pocket doors from the passage into the living room and from the living room into the dining room; in both cases there were glass panes in the upper part of the doors.

The focal point of the living room was a fireplace on the west side wall; the fireplace surround consisted of reddish-brown ceramic tiles. The mantel shelf was also tile, though just beneath this was a classical egg-and-dart molding. Both the dining room and the kitchen, which was on the other side of a pantry, were wider than the rooms in front of them (as the side walls were pushed outward) but not as deep. The dining room had a fire-place on the back wall, as did the bedroom above it, which was presumably the master bedroom. Upstairs were four bedrooms, those on the west wider than those on the east, echoing the arrangement downstairs. Beyond the kitchen was a two-story frame porch; the upper story of this space certainly served as a sleeping porch. At the back of the lot was a one-story frame garage.

This side-passage plan is more old-fashioned than the exterior. As a native of Mobile William Colgin would have been very familiar with side-passage houses, now sometimes known as the Southern town house, which could be found there and in New Orleans, Galveston, Houston, and even Waco at the Earle-Harrison house. (Jennie could also have seen such houses in St. Louis.)

In 1912 William, 52, and Jennie, 42, anticipated being empty nesters in the near future. Merchant and Irwin had both become doctors and moved into their own arts-and-crafts-inspired

   Chapter Two

houses at 2611 and 2621 Austin. Monette and Willie were still at home. William may well have suspected (rightly) that Jennie would outlive him by a substantial number of years and wanted to make sure she had a nice, newer house in which to live.

By 1920 the household had actually expanded. Monette married Manton Hannah, a native of Paris (Texas, that is). Manton was a college-educated civil engineer who worked on county roads. (Monette had two years of college herself.) Their first and only child, Manton Jr., was an infant in 1920. William Colgin Sr. died in 1923, but Jennie lived until 1956, dying at age 94. Generally, the family had one live-in servant, who was usually an African American woman. In 1910 that was Dina Pease, 21, who was a general servant; in 1930 it was Estelle Allen, 20, who worked as the cook. In this time period having one servant was upper middle class, while upper-class families would have two, usually a woman and a man.

The anticipated cost of the house had been $8,000. Estimates of its value in subsequent censuses indicated that they had come close to hitting that mark and that over time it retained that value well. In 1930 Jennie estimated the value at $10,000; in 1940, despite a decade of depression, it had only dropped to $9,000. Newer houses in Castle Heights or other trendy neighborhoods were often valued at two or three times that, but such Roaring Twenties valuations usually gave way to half of that ten years later. ■

141. Mrs. Mettie Fisher House

910 N. Eighteenth Street / 1912

A stylish American Foursquare, this house had a brick-veneered first floor and a stucco-veneered second floor. As on most Foursquares, the roof was hipped; here there were two dormers with semicircular roofs, one facing Eighteenth Street and the other, the side street. The front porch originally was only in front of the house; sometime after 1950 it was expanded to both sides. On the south side, away from the side street, was a porte cochere. The porch roof was supported by three brick piers, which were unevenly placed. A pier lined up with both the front corners of the house; the third was off-center to the right so that the entrance was framed by two piers, and the larger portion of the porch was enclosed by a low wall.

The floor plan probably had direct entry into a living hall with staircase; to the left was the living room, with a set of three windows in the front wall and a fireplace on the side wall. On the side street there was a secondary, round-arched door, given a bit of shelter by an arched roof.

141. Mrs. Mettie
Fisher House

Even the glass in this door appears to be original. In the rear was a two-story outbuilding, garage below and apartment above.

Mettie Fisher was the widow of John Henry Fisher of Colorado County. Fisher fought in the Confederate Army at the Battle of Vicksburg as part of Waul's Texas Legion; after the war he worked as a lumber dealer. John and Mettie were ardent Baptists and moved to Waco in August 1901 so that their only son, Johnnie, could attend Baylor University. They bought a house at 824 Speight, conveniently located near the campus, pushed it to the back of the lot, and rotated it to face the side street (now 1620 S. Ninth Street). The Fisher family lived there while building a two-story late-Victorian house on the front of the lot (now replaced by a dreary apartment building).

In May 1902, just as the new house was coming to completion, John Henry Fisher was electrocuted by a fallen telephone wire. John had been 61, Mettie was 44, and Johnnie was 17. Mettie, now a widow, owned the house free and clear and could afford two African American servants, one working in the house, the other in the yard, and sometimes took in boarders. In 1912 Mettie and Johnnie moved to this house. The area beyond this was thinly settled. At that point the only other house on that block of Colonial was a frame house on the north side of the street, which was later replaced with an apartment house. In fact, at this time the street name was not Colonial but Reservoir because of the water-gathering tank that used to be where Seley Park is today.

As with the house on Speight, Mettie Fisher owned this house free and clear with no need for a mortgage. John B. Fisher tried a number of professions, including groceries, real estate, automobile supplies and tires, and life insurance, before becoming an officer of the Pioneer Building & Loan Association, eventually becoming chairman of the board. He married Eula Belle Berly, a Beaumont native who attended Baylor in 1901–02. They had two children, John B. Jr. and Mary Lucille Fisher. John Jr. followed the example of his parents, attending Baylor in the late 1930s; he became a lawyer. All that time they were living with Mettie, who died in 1939. The family continued to live in the house for many years. ■

142. Dave and Jennie Hawtof House

1525 Austin Avenue   /   Circa 1912

A furniture dealer named Dayton Taylor and his wife, Mary, lived at this address in 1910 and 1911, but this may have been in an earlier frame Victorian house, noted on the 1899 Sanborn Map. The present building was definitely the long-term home of merchant Dave Hawtof; his wife, Jennie; and their family, who were living in this house by 1913. Dave was born in Minsk, the capital of Belarus (sometimes known as "Little Russia") in 1865. His family came to the United States around 1877, when he was 12. They landed at Boston and soon moved to Philadelphia. Dave left his family behind (including three sisters and a brother) and moved to Waco around 1889.

His first job was as a grocery clerk, but he soon owned his own dry goods store on the south side of the Square. He married around 1896, and he and Jennie had four children. The family was Jewish and attended Temple Rodef Sholom. Dave also was a Mason and a Shriner. Around the time this house was built, poor health forced Dave to retire, but he still dabbled in real estate. In 1930 they even had a live-in servant, Mary Kucera, a native of Texas but of Czech ancestry.

142. Dave and Jennie Hawtof House

Dave died in 1933; his pallbearers included Louie Migel, Asher Sanger, Alex Sanger, Leo Bruck, and Edmund Bruck. He was buried at Hebrew Rest. Jennie continued to live in the house with her eldest son, Emanuel; his wife, Mildred; and son, David. Emanuel was a geologist, which presumably meant he worked in the emerging oil industry. After World War II he worked in real estate and loans, with an office in the Liberty Building on Austin Avenue. Both of Jennie's daughters married and moved to Milwaukee.

Although this house has suffered from an unfortunate and very prominent addition, it is one of the oldest surviving houses on Austin Avenue. A classic American Foursquare, it was built of brick and had two stories with a hipped roof. There was a one-story front porch and a porte cochere on the right side. Trios of windows were used on the left side of the ground floor and the front and side elevations of the upper floor. The curving brackets supporting the hipped dormer window have also survived intact. By 1926 there was a small outbuilding at the northwest corner of the lot and a larger garage at the northeast corner. At a later date part of the garage was converted into an apartment.

But when this stretch of the avenue switched from residential to retail, a new space was added, swallowing up the front lawn and the front porch. This crude addition has large plate-glass windows and blank side walls, pierced only by one door and two air-conditioning units. At the same time the porte cochere was removed and replaced with a cheap awning to match the one on the front. Amazingly, the nicely detailed square piers of the front porch still survive and could be easily restored to some level of dignity. ■

1421 Austin Avenue   /   Circa 1912

Although American Foursquares have their roots in the arts and crafts movement, they could easily be expanded with a porte cochere and sleeping porches and dressed up with neoclassical details. In this case the roof was classic Foursquare, but the façade was quite nuanced, with classical columns across the front porch and a doorway with an elliptical fanlight above. While many Foursquares have two front rooms and thus an off-center front door, this had a central hallway with an elliptical arch opening into the stair hall, and the walls of both front rooms project. Both front rooms were living rooms; the dining room was the right rear room and the kitchen the rear left room, with a pantry in between. The original brick fireplaces in the two rooms on the right were the most arts and crafts feature of the interior.

Tom Bush was a native of Southborough, Massachusetts, while his wife, Mary Adelaide, was a Texas native. Tom moved to Texas in 1898 and to Waco in 1902. He was a principal in Bush & Witherspoon, cotton exporters and traders, and later served as president of the Cotton Palace Association and as mayor of Waco. In 1920 the household include Tom, Mary, her two children by a previous marriage, and three African American servants. Ella Walker was the cook; Ida Lockett, the maid; and Earnest Hayward, the yard man. Tom died in 1940, but Mary continued to live in the house for decades. In 1976 McLennan County purchased the property and turned it into a halfway house. In 1994 it was acquired by Compassion Ministries, which slowly restored the house back to its original character. ◼

143. Tom and Mary Bush House

144. Wheatley-Corwin-Kindler House

2411 Lasker Avenue / Circa 1912

In the early 1910s Lasker Avenue grew to the west. This house was built between 1911 and 1913 as a rent house. The first occupant was a barber, William T. Wheatley; by 1916 the occupants were Charles and Rose (Atcheson) Corwin. Charles was a native of Kansas, while Rose was from Kaufman County, Texas, east of Dallas. Charles, a piano tuner by trade, worked for Thomas Goggin and Brother, the Galveston firm that had branches selling pianos across the eastern part of the state, including Waco. The Corwins lived in this house for several years.

By 1921 the house was occupied by Edward A. Kindler and his wife, Rose (Huber) Kindler. They were both born in Belleville, Illinois, but had moved to Waco by 1910. Edward had a high school education, while Rose attended through the sixth grade. Edward worked as an agent for the Langdon E. Luedde Insurance Company, a salesman for the W. D. Lacy Insurance Company, and as a salesman for the Southwestern Drug Company. When they moved into this house, Edward was 34 and Rose 31, and they had one son, Edward Jr., who was 8. (A second son, Langdon, arrived a few years later.) They also had two people rooming with them, which certainly helped pay the rent. In 1930 they were still renting, paying twenty-five dollars per month. By 1940 they could proudly report that they owned their own home without a mortgage, which they valued at $1,750. The Kindlers were Roman Catholic. St. Louis Roman Catholic Church was built nearby, but only in 1968, so the Kindlers had to go to St. Mary of the Assumption Catholic Church on Washington (see *Historic Buildings*, 14). Edward died in 1958, and Rose in 1971; they are buried in Waco Memorial Park.

Their house was a one-story Foursquare—that is, a bungalow with a steep hipped roof—which had a hipped-roof dormer on the front and the west side. The porch is inset beneath the main roof and runs all the way across the front. The four columns are square and are ornamented near the top in a manner typical of Foursquares and bungalows. Originally there was a nearly identical house at 2407; the main difference was that 2411 had a small inset back porch at the northeast corner, and 2407 at the northwest corner, so that they faced one another. In recent years the house has been fixed up, with all new windows, unpainted wooden shutters, and a bluish-gray coat of paint. In spite of such changes the original character of the house is still evident. ◼

144. Wheatley-Corwin-Kindler House

145. Clyde and Katherine Spencer Webb House
(Webb-Johnson House)

2407 Colcord Avenue   /   1912–13

This house and its neighbor at 2425 Colcord were built for members of the Spencer family and their spouses. The stay of Clyde Lee Webb and Katherine Spencer Webb was relatively short, but its new owners, Norwegian immigrants John and Jennie Johnson, would live there for many years.

Katherine Spencer was born in Dublin, Texas, but went away to study at the Gunston Hall School in Washington, D.C. This elite girls' school had been founded by Confederate veteran Beverly Randolph Mason, who named his school for the home of his great-grandfather, the Founding Father George Mason. The Spencer family moved from Dublin to Waco in 1909. When Kathy returned to Texas, she attended Baylor and then married Clyde Lee Webb.

Clyde was born in Fulton, Itawamba County, Mississippi, in 1887; his father died when Clyde was very young, and around 1893 his mother, Nannie (Austin) Webb, married Isaac Curtis, a traveling salesman for the lumber industry. In 1900 they were living in Sherman in North Texas; Clyde was 12, the youngest of three boys. Ten years later, Nannie was a widow again, and the family had moved to Waco. They were living on Blair Street: Nannie was 42 and twice widowed; Roy Webb, 24, and his wife, Frankie, already had a son, 4-year-old Charles; and Clyde was 22 and single. Both Roy and Clyde had found employment with the R. B. Spencer Lumber Company, and Clyde was particularly successful, as he won the hand of Kathy Spencer. Over the next few years Clyde's title at work alternated between "clerk" and the somewhat more exalted "private secretary."

On January 19, 1913, the *Waco Morning News* reported that Mrs. Nannie Webb Curtis and Mr. and Mrs. Clyde Webb were about to move into their new home. Obviously, this meant that most of the planning and construction happened in 1912. Like the Spencer house next door, this house was a Foursquare with a hipped roof and a wide front porch. While the Spencer house was later sheathed with synthetic siding, the Webb house retains its original clapboards. Though the Spencer house had a two-story wing on the east side, this house originally had a one-story side porch. This was later removed, but the door into the living room, which was flanked by side lights, is still visible.

The stairs were similar to those on the Spencer house at 2425, including the landing, which also opened into the back middle room, but these stairs turned to the rear of the house to reach the upper floor. Like the house next door, the living room had a fireplace on the side wall, but the room did not extend all the way to the back of the house. On the left were the dining room, the pantry, and the kitchen. At a later date the kitchen was dramatically enlarged to the west. The master bedroom was over the living room; two more bedrooms with a shared bathroom were on the west, and a fourth bedroom was over the front part of the entrance hall. Thus, Nannie Curtis could have her choice from three bedrooms.

In July 1917 Clyde learned that he had been drafted to serve in World War I. On returning from the war, Clyde resumed working for R. B. Spencer. However, by 1921 they were living not in this house but in the Crawford Apartments at 2000 Austin Avenue (see 154 in this book). Two

145. Clyde and Katherine Spencer Webb House (Webb-Johnson House)

years later they were living in the home of Kathy's mother at 1324 Columbus. Various city directories from the 1920s show them alternating between these two addresses, but by 1930 Clyde and Kathy were living in Houston. In that year he was the proprietor of an investment company, and ten years later he was president of a gas equipment company.

They returned to Waco in the early 1940s and lived at the Palm Court on Austin Avenue, the most upscale apartment house in town (see *Historic Homes*, 84). Clyde died in 1946, and Kathy the next year. Clyde's funeral was officiated by the minister from the Austin Avenue Methodist Church, suggesting that he had grown up a Methodist. When Kathy died, her body was taken to the home of her brother Harry, next to the house in which she had lived, until it was time for her funeral, which was officiated by the minister from her home church, Columbus Avenue Baptist. They were buried in Oakwood Cemetery.

Much longer-term owners were John and Jennie Christine (Olson) Johnson. Though they were both born in Norway, they immigrated separately, John around 1890 and Jennie in 1893. Apparently, they met in Waco and were married around 1895. Like many Norwegians, they were Lutheran and belonged to the First Lutheran Church, which was officially known as the Scandinavian Lutheran Church when it was founded in 1916 (see *Historic Buildings*, 5). They had four children, Olaf, Edwin, Ingeborg, and Gladys; the first three arrived two years apart, but Gladys arrived after a ten-year break from childbearing. Jennie's younger brother Gustav also moved from Norway to Waco. In fact, he lived with the Johnsons in his earliest years in Waco. John, Jennie, and family moved into this house in late 1920 or early 1921.

In his earlier years John called himself a carpenter, but his ability to organize large projects with many workmen led him to become a contractor. His big break came in 1910 when he won the contract to build the new Waco High School on Columbus, designed by Waller and Field of Fort Worth in association with Scott and Pearson of Waco (see *Historic Buildings*, 75). In the 1920s he worked closely with architect Milton W. Scott, building the Penland house on Park Avenue (see *Historic Homes*, 60), the Hilton Hotel (designed by Lang & Witchell of Dallas but supervised by Scott; see *Historic Buildings*, 60) and its dramatic enlargement (designed by Scott on his own), and the McDermott Motor Company Building at 1125 Washington (see *Historic Buildings*, 32). His last big project was Waco Hall on the Baylor campus, designed by Lang & Witchell with Harry L. Spicer as structural engineer (see *Historic Buildings*, 79).

Both Olaf and Edwin followed in their father's footsteps: in 1920 Olaf gave his occupation as architect and Edwin as carpenter. Apparently, they were both working for their father. (Like his brother-in-law, Gus Olson began as a carpenter and became a contractor.) Ten years later John gave no occupation, but Edwin now called himself a contractor, suggesting that he was doing most of the work on building Waco Hall. In fact, John died later in 1930. In 1940 Jennie was living in this house by herself, and she lived here until her death in 1946. ■

146. Harry L. and Bertie Spencer House

2425 Colcord Avenue   /   1913

This house and its neighbor at 2407 Colcord were built for members of the Spencer family and their spouses. Harry Lee Spencer was the eldest son of Richard B. Spencer, who opened a lumberyard in Waco in 1909, and Mary Catherine Lattimore Spencer. The Spencers were Baptists and bought the old Sam Sanger house next to Columbus Avenue Baptist Church. Harry attended Baylor University and discovered a lifelong passion for music. He played the piano and especially the pipe organ at church. He directed the choir at Columbus Avenue for forty years, playing the organ for forty-eight. After some additional musical studies in New York City, Harry settled into a position at his father's company and married Bertie Harris of Fort Worth. They had one daughter, Mary K. Spencer. Harry was president of the board of Hillcrest Hospital, another Baptist institution. In addition to his extensive church and civic work, Harry was deeply involved with various Masonic organizations.

146. Harry L. and Bertie Spencer House

Harry and Bertie took out a permit to build their house on March 25, 1913, little more than eight weeks after his sister Kathy and her husband, Clyde Webb, moved into their house next

door. Their houses were extremely similar. They were essentially American Foursquares, with a hipped roof and a broad front porch framed by square brick piers. (The cast-iron posts on 2425 most likely were inserted in the 1950s.) A two-story wing, also under a hipped roof, projected on the right (east) side. Originally the first floor was open but was enclosed to make a sunroom sometime after 1950. More recently the house was wrapped in synthetic siding, which does not quite capture the rhythm of the original wooden clapboards. In 1913 the building was expected to cost $3,500; by 1930 the family estimated its value at $10,000.

Some Foursquares have two front rooms and an off-center door, but Harry and Bertie opted for a house that retained formal symmetry. Other Foursquares with centered doors had a narrow central passage (such as the Corey house at 1112 Clay), but Harry and Bertie chose a shallow, squarish foyer with the staircase starting on the left side of the back wall. To the right was the living room, which extended the entire depth of the house. A fireplace was on the side wall; to the right was a window and to the left, a door onto the open porch. To the left of the foyer was the dining room, and behind this were a pantry and the kitchen. Additional support space was behind the staircase. Out back, against the property line, was a two-car garage and a small apartment for a servant. No one was living there in 1920, but in 1930 there were two servants in the household, both white: Neta Lerche and John H. Upton.

After World War II Harry's sister Ethel and her husband, Wilton Lanning Sr., who had just returned from fighting in the war, bought the house across Twenty-Fifth Street at 2501. This house was demolished sometime between 1950 and 2000. ◾

147. Allan and Frances Sanford House (Sanford-Barrett House)

2114 Austin Avenue / 1913

This was a classic American Foursquare, though somewhat elaborated. The front block was quite squarish, with a hipped roof and a front dormer. Above was a hipped roof. But the house expanded to both sides and to the rear. (In addition, there was a one-story side porch on the west side—the original driveway ran past this porch, which served as a secondary entrance for visitors arriving by car.) The main roof and the dormer roof both had exposed rafter ends, an indication that this was a house in sympathy with the arts and crafts movement. The one-story, single-bay front porch was supported by two Doric columns, a Colonial Revival touch; above this was a wooden balustrade, now replaced with an iron railing. The house was built of tile blocks, which were stuccoed over, and had a tile roof. This was as fireproof as you could get in 1913. At the rear was a two-story structure, with a two-car garage on the first floor and apartment above.

Inside the front door was the living room, which stretched to the west end of the house. On the back wall was the fireplace, and to each side were double French doors. The French doors on the left opened into the dining room; the one on the right, into a smaller room with similar

147. Allan and Frances Sanford House (Sanford-Barrett House)

wainscoting. This room had windows and a pair of French doors that opened onto a covered porch; another pair of French doors from the living room opened onto an uncovered porch. To the left of the living room was a smaller front room, behind which was a compact staircase. At the back right corner was the kitchen, which connected to the dining room. Across the rear was a living porch, and above was a sleeping porch, now enclosed.

The house was built for Allan D. Sanford and Frances (Brodie) Sanford and their son, Allan Jr. Both Allan and Frances were natives of Tennessee. Allan was an 1893 graduate of the University of Texas, where he received his law degree. He served as city attorney for Waco and in 1903 was elected mayor. When this house was being built, he was general attorney for the Amicable Life Insurance Company, which meant he had an office in what is now known as the ALICO Building. Sanford later served as president of the Texas State Bar Association.

In May 1916 ex-mayor Sanford was concerned about the likelihood that Jesse Washington would be lynched for the murder of Lucy Fryer of Robinson. He was said to have secured a promise from the people of Robinson that they would not participate in a lynching and spoke to Sheriff S. S. Fleming and Judge Richard I. Munroe, urging them to stop talk of a lynching, but no promise was forthcoming from Wacoans who favored a lynching, and the sheriff made no attempt to protect Washington after he was found guilty.

In 1917 the house was rented to Edward and Katherine Rotan. They had sold their Columbus Avenue mansion to the Dossett family and were planning a new one for 2425 Austin Avenue. The Sanfords were back in the house by 1919 and were joined by a second family, William and Lena Kelly. William was the manager of the Edwards-Orand Transfer Company. Living in the apartment out back was Eliza Prather, a 60-year-old African American woman, who was a servant in the home. (In the late 1920s the Sanfords ended up living at 2420 Colcord Avenue, the former home of Artemas Roberts, the founder of the Amicable Life Insurance Company; see *Historic Homes*, 34.)

By 1921 the house had a new owner, Edward C. Barrett, vice president of the Cooper Grocery Company. Barrett was single, but he was joined in the house by two unmarried sisters, Mary and Lula. Lula lived there until her death in 1937 at age 64, and Mary until her death in 1948 at age 80. Their older brother, Edward, outlived them both, dying in 1952 at age 86. They are all buried together in Oakwood Cemetery.

This house was built on a high-status lot; not only was it on Austin Avenue, always an elite Waco address, but next door to the east was Pat M. Neff. A native of Coryell County, Neff had already served two terms in the Texas House, the second of those as speaker. Returning to Waco, he was elected county attorney in 1906; he built a house at 2110 Austin around that time. Little is known about that house, which must have been a late version of the Queen Anne style. In the early 1920s the house was rented because Neff had been elected governor of Texas and he and his family were living in the Governor's Mansion in Austin. Apparently living in the mansion made their old house on Austin Avenue feel a bit dowdy, as in June 1925 Neff hired Waco contractor N. A. Palmer to give the house a Colonial Revival makeover for $6,500. It was completed in time to be featured in the *Waco Chamber of Commerce News* for April–May 1926. In 1930 the Barretts estimated the value of their house at $3,000, which was very low; the Neffs estimated that their house, of a similar size, was worth $20,000. ■

148. J. Edward and Laura Brown House

2304 Colcord Avenue / 1914

The baronial house of Waco ice man Alfred Abeel (see *Historic Homes*, 36) has been erroneously called the "Cottonland Castle," but this house, built for a cotton buyer and his family, can correctly be known as the "Cottonland Foursquare." Its original owners were Jacob Edward Brown and his wife, Laura Lyle Brown. J. Ed Brown was a native of Anderson County, South Carolina, who came to Texas by 1900 and opened a dry goods store in Hood County. He hired a clerk, Arthur Lyle, and ended up marrying Arthur's older sister, Laura. The Lyles were native Texans with Tennessee roots. Laura had a college education, while Ed had completed two years of high school. They had two children: a daughter, Daisy, and a son, Edward Vandiver. They came to Waco around 1910, when Ed and Laura were both 40, Daisy was 12, and Van was 8. Ed quickly established himself as a cotton buyer; his office was on the twelfth floor of the new Amicable

148. J. Edward and Laura Brown House

Building, now known as the ALICO. This house was built in 1914; for a year it was rented by a traveling salesman, Edwin L. Thomas (who sometimes sold barber supplies, sometimes ice); his wife, Flossie May; and his son, Harry. The Brown family were in the house by July 1916 and owned it for the rest of their lives.

In 1920 the household included their two children plus Daisy's husband, Thomas Hardin, who was a traveling salesman, and Laura's mother, Mary Lyle. Daisy and Tom moved to Fort Worth later in the 1920s. Van, having graduated from Waco High in 1917, entered Rice Institute, recently opened in Houston. He played on the basketball team and was elected team captain his sophomore year. In 1920 Rice nominated him for a Rhodes Scholarship, though it is unclear whether he received one. In the mid-1920s he did spend a year in Europe; once back in the United States he lived in New York City. During the early 1930s Ed and Laura moved to their farm near Hearne, which they called Goodland Farm. While they were gone, they rented the house on Colcord to Dr. and Mrs. J. Z. Sexton, but they were back in this house by June 1934.

The core of the house was a two-story square block with a hipped roof; projecting forward was a dormer, which also had a hipped roof. On the right (west) side is a wing with another hipped roof, open on the first floor, forming a porte cochere, and enclosed on the second. This was not terribly symmetrical, though there was a one-story porch on the other side. Some Foursquares could be dressed up in colonial garb, as was the case with the slightly earlier Roberts-Sanford house at 2420 Colcord (see *Historic Homes*, 34); here the four square piers supporting the roof of the one-story front porch and the two at the outer ends of the porte cochere and the east side porch seem to have a sober arts and crafts simplicity to them. Like many Foursquares, their house did not have a central passage. Rather, there were two front rooms, an entry hall on the right, and a living room on the left. Behind the living room was the dining room and then the kitchen. As in 2420 Colcord, the only fireplace was in the entry hall.

The two-story frame garage apartment, which was a very early two-car garage, is largely original. In 1920 it was occupied by an African American couple, Earl and Willie Smith. Earl was the yard man while Willie was the cook. By 1940 Earl had passed away, but Willie continued to work for the family as housekeeper. She paid four dollars a month in rent. She had attended college for two years, which gave her fewer years in the classroom than Laura but more than Ed.

The house is reasonably intact, although the front door has been replaced and stained glass of a recent vintage has been inserted in many of the windows. ■

149. George and Eleanor Perry House

2000 N. Fourth Street / Circa 1914–15

George Albert Perry, who went by Bert, had banking in his blood. He was born in Hamilton, northwest of Waco, and his first job was at the Hamilton National Bank, where his father was the cashier. Bert married a Hamilton girl, Eleanor Boynton. In 1910, they had been married a year and a half, and Bert was working as an assistant cashier at the local bank, but by 1913 the young couple had moved to Waco. Bert had secured a job at the First National Bank of Waco, starting as bookkeeper but moving steadily to teller, assistant cashier, cashier, and finally vice president. They were Presbyterians, and Bert was a Shriner and a Mason.

All of the houses in this block faced Cameron Park, created in 1910. (This part of the park was later chosen to become the Cameron Park Zoo, now shielded by a wall of bamboo.) Bert and Eleanor built a classic bungalow. A large porch was on the left, and a one-story front room was on the right. Behind this was a two-story section that seemed to pop up from the house. (This is sometimes known as an "airplane bungalow," but this was not a term that Bert and Eleanor would have known.) The slope of the roof on the front porch echoed that of the two-story section, and both projected out beyond the side walls and were supported with brackets. Even the striped awnings were popular in Waco at this time. ■

149. George and Eleanor Perry House

150. Harvey Mac and Willie Richey House

1825 Colonial Avenue   /   Circa 1915

This house was built for a well-known Waco attorney and his family. Both Harvey MacGaughey Richey and Willie Camille Seley Richey were Waco natives. Willie was the daughter of William Winthrop Seley, president of the Waco State Bank and of the Seley-Early Grain Company and an officer of the Waco Savings Bank. The Richey house was the closest thing in Waco to an example of the Prairie style, the arts and crafts variant created by Frank Lloyd Wright and other architects in Chicago in the years before World War I.

Harvey and Willie both attended Baylor, albeit ten years apart. In addition, Harvey attended law school at the University of Texas. In 1913 Harvey was a justice of the peace and notary, with an office in the new McLennan County Courthouse. Harvey and Willie married around 1912 and had three children: Harvey Jr., Jessie Van (named for her maternal grandmother), and Frank. By 1916 Harvey was a lawyer and notary with an office on the fifteenth floor of the new Amicable Building (ALICO), and the family was living in this house. Harvey lived until 1967, and Willie until 1969.

In the Roy E. Lane Papers at Baylor is a photograph of a perspective drawing of this house, which strongly suggests that Lane was the architect. It was two stories but low slung with a hipped roof. At the west end was a two-story wing with an open porch below and a sleeping porch (enclosed but with three windows on the front and six on the side) and beyond that a one-story porte cochere. Originally the walls had a veneer of stucco, and the chimney facing Colonial was unpainted, which would have provided a contrast both in color and texture. The angled mullions in the upper sash of the windows were quite distinctive.

The one-story garage with hipped roof at the rear included quarters for servants, always an African American couple. In 1920 it was Cicero and Laura Wiggins (he worked as a janitor, and she as a cook) and in 1930 Vandy and Lula Parker (also a janitor and a cook). In 1940 Nathaniel and Irine Jones were living there. He cared for the lawn, while she was a housekeeper. The house backs up to Seley Park, which is named in honor of Willie Richey's father. ◼

150. Harvey Mac and Willie Richey House

151. Jesse J. and Jessie Dean House

3101 Maple Avenue   /   Circa 1915

This two-story frame Foursquare was built for the developer of the Dean Addition (now Dean Highlands), Jesse J. Dean, and his wife, Jessie. (As if the similarity in their names was not confusing enough, they named their firstborn son Jesse Jr.) Jessie was the daughter of Lee Trice, a farmer who was a nephew of William Berry Trice, the prominent Waco contractor and brick maker. Dean ran his real estate office from the twelfth floor of the Amicable Life Insurance Building (now known as the ALICO). In addition to developing the neighborhood, in 1916 Dean donated land at Thirtieth and Herring for the Central Texas Baptist Sanitarium, which was later known as Hillcrest Baptist Hospital. (The earliest part of the hospital was built in 1918.)

The Dean house was one of the earliest in the neighborhood: they were living there by the time of the 1916 city directory. In 1920 they had six children; by 1930 there were eleven. The simple box of the Foursquare was broken up by porches on the front and both sides. The western side porch was open on the ground floor but contained another room above. As was the case with many Foursquares, the front door was not centered but opened into an entry hall that was one of two front rooms. The staircase was not in the entry hall but in the space behind it, and the kitchen was beyond that. The left front room was the living room, which had double doors opening into the dining room and then a breakfast room. At the rear of the property was a two-story frame building, which was a two-car garage on the first floor and an apartment on the second. Often such an apartment provided housing for servants, but by 1930 the Deans may have been able to use it for some of their eleven children. ■

151. Jesse J. and Jessie Dean House

212 Dallas Street / Circa 1916

This home and the one just to the left were built for Milo and Florence Wilkins. Milo was a druggist, and in partnership with H. Swan Forman he had a drugstore on the corner of Elm Avenue and Dallas Street. The earlier house is the late Victorian at 210 Dallas. This older house had a projecting front room on the right and a porch on the left. Above was a steep hipped roof with two gables in front. Both were nearly equilateral, with an upper triangle within the larger one; both had a sunburst motif above and a pattern of shingles below. Originally, there was a back porch as well. Sometime between 1926 and 1950 a store was built onto the house, taking over all but a tiny portion of the porch and projecting all the way to the street.

After more than a decade in this house, Milo and Florence decided to build another house next door. Although the footprint was slightly smaller than that of their old house, it was a full two stories. It was a fairly typical American Foursquare, a style that was quite popular in Waco. From the front it seems to be a two-story box, with a pyramidal roof above. However, this Foursquare had some subtle differences: there were hipped roof dormers only on the front and right side, the front porch was only on the right side, and there was a bay window centered on the north side wall. (The porch has now been expanded across the entire front, with a compatible design.) The porch roof was held up by two square piers, to the side of which were Doric columns. Originally the roof was shingled, except for the porch, which was metal. The chimney on the right served a fireplace in the entry hall; the chimney on the left served both the front and back rooms. There was a one-story frame garage fronting on the side street (Rusk) and the alley; before 1950 this was replaced with a two-story frame structure, with a garage on the first floor and an apartment above. ■

152. Milo and Florence Wilkins House

153. Weathered-Vick-Barnes House

2220 Gorman Avenue   /   Circa 1916

Though most of the houses on this block of Gorman Avenue show the influence of the arts and crafts movement, this is the only one that is a canonical American Foursquare. Its footprint was not precisely square, but it was definitely boxy. Its roof and the roof of its wide dormer were hipped. While several other houses on the block had exposed rafter ends, the eaves of this house were neatly enclosed. The one-story porch had four boxy columns supporting its roof; these columns did not extend to the floor of the porch but landed upon a low, solid wall, which enclosed the space. To the rear was a two-story porch, doubtless to provide a sleeping porch on

153. Weathered-
Vick-Barnes House

the upper level. At the very rear of the lot was a one-story garage, the only garage on the block not to have two stories and thus an apartment for a servant.

The front door apparently opened into the left front room, which was both a stair hall and a room of living. The actual living room was the right front room, with the fireplace on the back wall so that its chimney could also serve the fireplace in the dining room behind.

The original owners and occupants were Charles A. Weathered and his wife, Minnie. Charles was the president of the Waco Motor Co. Inc. and was also involved in real estate and an abstract company. His office in 1923 was in the Bankers Trust Building at 526–528 Austin Avenue (see *Historic Buildings*, 24). The Weathereds were gone by 1919, and by 1923 they were living at 1821 Morrow, a bungalow designed by Milton W. Scott, where they lived for many years (see *Historic Homes*, 47). The house at 2220 Gorman became a rent house; in the early 1920s it was rented by Cornelius R. Myers and his wife, Willie. Cornelius was a general yard master for the railroads.

Around 1925 Kyle Vick, an attorney, and his wife, Lucille, purchased the house. Vick served for a number of years as a judge in the County Court at Law for McLennan County. When he was in private practice, he officed on the fifteenth floor of the Amicable Life Building, what is now known as the ALICO Building. In 1936 the Vick family moved, and 2220 became the residence of a young doctor and his wife: Maurice Barnes and Lavonia Jenkins Barnes, known as Bobbie. They had just moved to Waco from Coleman in West Texas. Dr. Barnes also had an office in the Amicable Building, but two floors down from Judge Vick. Bobbie Barnes became an important leader in the historic preservation movement in Waco, encouraging the creation of historic house museums and, later, the creation of the Historic Waco Foundation—now known as Historic Waco. The Barnes's stay was brief, for by 1940 they were living at 414 W. 120th Street in New York City, just across Amsterdam Avenue from the campus of Columbia University. Dr. Barnes was in private medical practice while continuing his medical education. (For their post–World War II house in Waco, see 206 in this book.)

Meanwhile, back in Waco, the house at 2220 Gorman was being rented by Harry and Fay Gorman. Harry was a salesman at a lumber company, and they paid forty-three dollars a month in rent. Harry and Fay had two daughters: Kathleen, 24, was a college graduate and a public school teacher; and Suzanne, 18, was a college freshman and a file clerk at a university, presumably Baylor. Perhaps the one-story garage was adapted as an apartment, because in 1940 Mattie White was living at 2220 Rear. She was a Louisiana native, a 42-year-old African American, and the family servant. She paid four dollars a month in rent for her quarters. ◼

2000 Austin Avenue / 1916

This apartment house is the earliest of three designed by Milton W. Scott. Soon after the completion of the Crawford Apartments he designed the Terrace Gardens Apartments on North Fourth Street (see 156 in this book), and in 1920 he designed the Palm Court Apartments just across Austin from the Crawford Apartments, where R. T. Dennis was his client (see *Historic Homes*, 84).

The apartment house was named for the man who developed it, Wilbur F. Crawford. A native of Illinois, Crawford was in Waco by 1916, when he was working as a solicitor (that is, a salesman) for the Texas Lumber & Loan Company and rooming one block east of this site at 1824 Austin. Crawford was only 27 when this building was completed, but Texas Lumber & Loan provided most of the building materials and plumbing fixtures.

Crawford hired Milton W. Scott to design the complex. Scott had worked for many years as a draftsman for W. W. Larmour, then in partnership with Glen Allen, designing the Artesian Manufacturing and Bottling Co. (see *Historic Buildings*, 43) and the First Baptist Church (see *Historic Buildings*, 2). In the years around 1910 Scott partnered with T. Brooks Pearson, designing the Smith-Parker-Migel house (see *Historic Homes*, 33) and Shear-Callan house (demolished; see *Historic Homes*, p. 11) and supervising the construction of Waco High School, designed by Fort Worth architects Waller and Field. Soon he was practicing on his own.

Crawford wanted a building holding ten apartments with an adjacent two-story garage that could also house servants. Four would have seven rooms, two would have six rooms, and four would have four rooms. The building was to have hardwood floors in most rooms and a tile floor in the bathroom. All stoves were to use natural gas, as did the hot-water boiler in the basement. All apartments would have a telephone, which was quite a novelty. The six- and four-room apartments had Murphy beds, which disappeared into the wall. Each apartment featured a sleeping porch or sunroom. The total cost was expected to be around $40,000.

Scott incorporated all these features into a two-story frame building covered with a veneer of stucco. This was not as expensive as a brick veneer, and the roof was covered with wooden shingles rather than fireproof slate. The building was not as stylish as the Tudor Revival Palm Courts; apparently Crawford gave Scott the mandate to focus on interior amenities rather than exterior detailing. The building was J-shaped, with a short façade on Austin Avenue and a longer façade on Nineteenth Street. The design incorporated numerous windows, allowing for light-filled rooms. Each apartment had a mix of casement and sash windows—apparently the casements were for the sleeping porches. Originally the entrance on Austin Avenue had a canvas awning, a feature that became very popular in Waco in the 1910s and 1920s, though that was later replaced with a simple shed roof. The matching garage, with room for five cars, was at the back of the lot. Above were rooms for six servants. Each servant had his or her own room, but they were expected to share one bathroom.

The contractors for the job were Bruyere & Ripley, who had recently built the Edward and Amelia Corey house at 1112 Clay and the Florence Delaney house at 707 N. Nineteenth at the back of the Losavio lot (see *Historic Homes*, 40 and 52). Samuel S. Ripley had been a carpenter

in Waco, but for this job he partnered with one or more members of the Bruyere family. Both Edgar H. and Horace A. Bruyere were experienced carpenters and contractors.

The early occupants of these apartments tended to be white middle-class to upper-middle-class professionals. Willard Wigley worked for the R. T. Dennis Furniture Company; his wife, Florence, was a daughter of R. T. Dennis, who lived across the street at 1923 Austin and who built the Palm Court Apartments at 2005 Austin. Edward Tobey and his wife, Celia, lived at the Crawford; Edward was the founder and superintendent of a business college on Fourth Street. Jesse Penix and his wife, Alvera, lived here as well; he worked for the Treasury Department as a bank examiner. Some occupants were passing through on the way to their own single-family home; this included Sidney and Isabel Davis, Grady and Hazel Yates, and Willard and Florence Wigley (see *Historic Homes*, 92, 93, and 72).

In 1919 Gus H. Pape and Eleanor "Nell" Jurney Pape lived in the Crawford. Gus was vice president of Wilson, Nabors & Pape, who were cotton exporters; in 1923 he created a new firm, Pape, Williams and Company. Pape was a native of Germany, and he and Nell traveled extensively. They saw the Crawford Apartments as a pied-à-terre in Waco; at other times they lived in the Palm Court or the Roosevelt Hotel. After Gus died, Nell became a leading Waco philanthropist and funded the preservation of the Earle-Harrison house (see *Historic Homes*, 3).

Wilbur Crawford remained a leader of the Waco business community for many decades. After World War I he began to sell army surplus, opening more than forty stores. Working with the government led him to open a factory making tents, cots, and other goods (see *Historic Buildings*, 48). In 1957, when Riverside Drive, connecting downtown Waco to Cameron Park, had been damaged by chronic flooding, Crawford repaired the road with his own crew and machinery. He also paved North Twenty-Fifth Street from Maple Avenue to Herring Avenue at his own expense—his home was at 2801 Herring (demolished). He also developed Franklin Center, the seemingly endless strip of one-story commercial spaces that stretched from Thirty-Second Street to Thirty-Eighth Street. Like the Crawford Apartments, these shops were not fancy, just functional. ◼

155. Joe and Rose Snaman House

905 N. Eighteenth Street   /   Circa 1916

Around 1916 this house was built for newlyweds Joe and Rose Snaman. A veneer of stucco covered a wooden frame; it was one of Waco's best examples of the Mission style. The hipped roof had exposed rafter ends in the manner of the arts and crafts movement and originally had a front porch with wide semicircular openings, matching the arch on the porte cochere. The curvilinear parapet above the entrance onto the porch was echoed in the parapet above the single dormer on the roof. The porch was removed in May 2008, and the house was put on the market in its debased condition. The front door had little to do with the Mission style, instead having an elliptical fanlight and side lights, typical of the early Neoclassical style often called Federal. A second entrance was under the porte cochere. However, the front door led directly into the living room, as would be expected in a bungalow or Mission-style house. All windows were casements and featured numerous square panes of glass.

Joe was a native of Russia and immigrated sometime between 1896 and 1900. He and his brother Harry arrived in Waco around 1912. Their first venture was the Texas Garment Company, which sold ladies' furnishings (that is, clothing) wholesale. Joe (then known as Jacob) was president, and H. Jaffe of Fort Worth was vice president and perhaps a silent partner. The business was at 612 Washington (now a parking lot), which was also Joe's residence. Joe and Harry also ran the St. Charles Hotel—perhaps this was Harry's responsibility. The partnership ended abruptly in 1913 when Harry passed away at age 36.

Joe rearranged his business affairs, creating Snaman & Co., which sold ladies' furnishings—now retail—out of a store at 507 Austin Avenue. (Later he added ladies' hats to his merchandise.) He married Rose Cohen, who was born in Missouri, but her father, Jacob Samuel Cohen, had

emigrated from Russia, and her mother, Yetta Kolber Cohen, was born in Vienna, Austria. Jacob ran a saloon somewhat incongruously named the Skating Rink, which was at 112 S. Second, just off the Square. Yetta died in 1916, just as this house was being finished, and Jacob died in Chicago in 1921.

In 1920 Joe and Rose were comfortably settled in this house and had been joined by a daughter, named Yetta for her maternal grandmother. In this year Joe was 39; Rose, 26; and Yetta Frances, 2 and a half. Business was good enough that the family could hire a live-in maid, Ethel Pettis. She was a 22-year-old African American and a native of Texas, as were both her parents. She was also divorced; many live-in servants were unmarried, divorced, or widowed. By 1923 Joe had thirteen employees, most of them women. There were two department managers and five salesclerks. One woman worked as a fitter, and two others did alterations. Even the bookkeeper was a woman. The only male employees were a man in charge of the credit department (who was white) and an African American porter.

Ten years later the family no longer had a live-in servant; they were, however, the proud owners of a radio. They estimated the value of the house at $15,000, which was less than many newer houses in Castle Heights but nevertheless a tidy sum. The family was still in this house in 1940. With the Great Depression dragging on, Rose was now working outside the home as a salesclerk at the store downtown. Yetta was 22 and still living at home, but she now went by her middle name, Frances. Also in the household was Rose's older sister, Sarah Cohen. Joe Snaman died in 1959, and Rose died in 1987. They are buried in Hebrew Rest Cemetery with Rose's parents.

The Appell house, just across Blair Street (see 179 in this book), and the Snaman house were featured together in the *Waco Chamber of Commerce News* in 1926, a sure sign of having arrived in Waco society. ◼

155. Joe and Rose Snaman House

156. Terrace Court (later Terrace Gardens) Apartments

611–617 N. Fourth Street   /   1916–17

In 1899 this site was occupied by four houses: on one lot was a two-story brick house (part of what is now 617), on the lot to the south was a one-story frame Victorian house, and just beyond that, where there is a parking lot today, were another two frame houses. The two-story brick house was the homestead of Thomas Jefferson Womack and his wife, Mary. In the early twentieth century the house was occupied by Rosa E. Smith, a widow who ran a boarding house, and then by Harry Novich, who sold crockery—china, glass, and queensware—from his shop at 509 Austin. Next door was the one-story frame Victorian house of Alfred and Sadie Abeel, designed by W. W. Larmour; around 1911 Alfred and Sadie decided to go large and commissioned Roy E. Lane to design them a castle at 3300 Austin Avenue (see *Historic Homes*, 36).

156. Terrace Court
(later Terrace Gardens)
Apartments

The well-known Waco architect Milton W. Scott had acquired all three lots by mid-1915. He moved into the brick house and in short order got to work creating apartments around a grassy courtyard. (He took out a building permit for the first four cottages, to cost $10,000, in June 1915.) At first it was known as Scott's Court or Scott's Apartments, but by 1921 the name was Terrace Court. Scott enlarged the extant brick house, creating two units down and two units up. The original one-story porch was demolished, and two two-story porches were created so that each apartment would have a sleeping porch.

Scott then built a two-story frame house covered with stucco, roughly where the Abeel house had been. (One wonders if Scott felt a pang of guilt or two for demolishing a house by his old boss Larmour.) Two two-story sleeping porches related it to the brick house across the way. These two houses became the upper parts of a U-shaped configuration and were closest to Fourth Street. Kate Edmond, in the *Waco News-Tribune*, suggested that Scott had designed a Southern California "bungalow court." Behind the stuccoed house were three bungalows, each stepping a little farther into the central courtyard. All three had a gabled front and an inset porch at the northwest corner, with pairs of classical columns; in back, the roofs were hipped, with inset porches at the southeast corner, though these have all been filled in. On the east side were two bungalows with mirror-image floor plans and façades; in between them was a two-story frame house. All had exposed rafter ends in good bungalow fashion. Finally, a simple two-story building behind the brick house on the north side also had two apartments upstairs and down.

The 1930 US Census took note of the rent paid on each unit. In the stucco building, renters paid either thirty-five or forty dollars a month (two of four units were vacant). Rents in the brick house were a bit less, ranging from twenty to thirty-five dollars a month—this even though one of the units was occupied by Milton and Ivy Scott and their two children, Margaret and John. Most of the bungalows were in the thirty-dollar range, although Apartment 1—the two-story bungalow on the east side—went for sixty dollars. In 1930 sixty-five dollars was the standard rent at the Palm Court on Austin Avenue; at Washington Terrace rents ranged from fifty-five to eighty dollars. Milton Scott proudly informed the census taker that the entire property was valued at $90,000, which was more valuable than any three houses on Austin Avenue. (That assessment would make it worth at least $1.2 million in today's dollars.) At the other end of the economic scale, a shotgun house one block to the west on Sixth Street rented for ten to twelve dollars a month, and an expanded shotgun for eighteen to twenty dollars.

Some residents of Terrace Court were upper middle class—physicians, attorneys, and cotton brokers. One well-to-do couple, Roy and Omah Albaugh, lived in Apartment F, the middle bungalow on the south side. They were new to town, and Roy was building his business, the Texas Fireproof Storage Company at 225 S. Eleventh Street (see *Historic Buildings*, 28). They were also working with Milton W. Scott on the design of a handsome house at 2201 Colcord (see *Historic Homes*, 75). But more residents were middle-middle class—salesmen and saleswomen, a linotype operator for the *Waco News-Tribune* and *Times-Herald*, managers of pharmacies and beauty shops, and the sergeant in charge of the US Army recruiting station. ■

157. Howard and Susie Dudgeon House

2200 Gorman Avenue   /   1916–17

In 1913 the only house in the 2200 block of Gorman was on the north side of the street, at 2225 Gorman, the home of Robert S. Ross, a real estate and insurance salesman. By 1916 the south side of the street was filled out with the houses of physicians and other professionals. This side of the street is quite intact and shows the many ways that architects and builders could use features from the arts and crafts movement in two-story houses.

The house of Howard and Susie Dudgeon was not only a corner lot; it was also nearly twice the size of any other lot on the block. The house sat under a hipped roof, with all rafter ends exposed in true Arts and Crafts style. A hipped roof dormer was on the back side of the house, and it would not be surprising if there had been one in front originally. The one-story front porch was not under the main roof, projecting forward from the front wall instead. Originally there was a small side porch facing Twenty-Second Street; the side door it sheltered is still present. There was also a two-story outbuilding, with a garage on the first floor and an apartment on the second, but this no longer exists. The chimney on the left side wall marked the living room inside.

Dr. Howard Dudgeon was a surgeon and physician in Waco for many years. The house next door at 2214 Gorman was also occupied by physicians: briefly by Charles W. Davis, then for many years by Warner I. Jenkins. Howard was 45 in 1920, and his wife, Susie, was 35. Their son, also named Howard, was 8. Living out back was their cook, Minna Wolf, 23, who was born in Texas but whose parents were from Germany. Ten years later the cook was Adeline Abel, 26, another Texan with Germanic roots. Presumably Stella Neumann, who was their cook in 1940, also had similar lineage. In 1930 they estimated the value of their home at $18,000; ten years later it was estimated to be worth $10,000, a typical decline in Depression-era Waco. ■

157. Howard and Susie Dudgeon House

2216 Gorman Avenue   /   1916–17

Like all houses on this side of the block, this one was built around 1916. It was built for A. R. (Alfred Randolph) Wilson and his wife, Gertrude. They were both natives of Virginia who moved to Waco around 1910 when he was 28 and she was 22. He was working for the Amicable Life Insurance Company as secretary and assistant actuary; his office was on the twenty-first floor of the building that bore his company's name (now the ALICO Building). At first, he and Gertrude lived at 1429 Washington; a year later they were at 1908 Fort (now a parking lot for Antioch Church), and by 1913 at 1919 Columbus (currently a vacant lot).

By 1917 they had built this house and moved into it. The house was two stories, with gables on the sides and a one-story porch with a forward-facing gable supported by brackets. Out back was a two-story garage. On this block five houses had a garage of two stories; only the one at 2220 Gorman, next door, was one story. The house was solidly middle class, but Randolph had higher aspirations for his career and for his house.

In 1920 the household consisted of Randolph, Gertrude, and their four daughters: Gertrude, 8; Mary, 6; and twins, Evelyn and Catharine, 4. This was the only census where an occupation was given for Gertrude Wilson: music teacher. By 1921 Randolph had become president of the life insurance company, a position he would hold for many years. By the end of 1923 Randolph and Gertrude were working with James P. Baugh and Duke Lovell to design a new house for the family. Their new house was clear evidence of what they did not like about their old house. The new house was on a very spacious lot between the Methodist Children's Home and Cameron Park, rather than the cramped lot on Gorman, and instead of a typical American Foursquare the new house was a rambling Tudor manse. And their new address alone spoke volumes: 600 Park Avenue (see *Historic Homes*, 87). ■

158. Randolph and Gertrude Wilson House

159. William and Sibyl Glasgow House

2226 Gorman Avenue / 1916–17

This house has many of the attributes of an American Foursquare, but it is clearly different from its Foursquare neighbor at 2220 Gorman. Both houses have a hipped roof with a hipped roof front dormer, but 2226 had exposed rafter ends. Moreover, its porch did not run across the entire façade but was partially inset on the left half and partially projected forward from the plane of the front wall. (The projecting portion also had exposed rafter ends.) From the porch, the door was on the right side wall, allowing direct entry into the living room. The fireplace on the side wall of this room was clearly marked on the exterior by the chimney. To the right of the chimney was a projection containing a door on the first floor and a pair of windows midway between the first and second floors. This feature, now known as a stair square, allowed some extra space for the landing of the stair and also provided the staircase with natural light.

The original owners were William and Sibyl Glasgow, both native Texans with roots in the Deep South. Will was born in West, just north of Waco, and was a civic leader there. He was one of the organizers of the National Bank of West; he worked as the cashier at the bank and later became president, a position he held even after he and Sibyl moved to Waco in 1915. In 1920, soon after this house was built, William was 53 and Sybil was 40. They had three teenage children, Minna, Bonibel, and William Jr. The family belonged to First Presbyterian Church in Waco (for that congregation's 1911 building, see *Historic Buildings*, 3). William Sr. frequently returned to West to visit friends and tend to bank business. He died of a heart attack in 1933 and was buried in the Bold Springs Cemetery in West next to a daughter who had died in infancy. The Reverend C. T. Caldwell of First Presbyterian officiated.

By 1940 the house on Gorman was being rented to Walter and Virginia Black. They had three young children, Alma, Walter, and Marcus. The family had been living in Dallas in 1935, and they moved to Waco so that Walter could take a job as a physician at the new Veterans Administration Hospital at 4800 Memorial Drive (see *Historic Buildings*, 69). The family had a housekeeper named Lillian Bishnow, an 18-year-old woman who lived in an apartment above the garage. ■

159. William and Sibyl Glasgow House

160. Buford-Fair House

1110 Elm Avenue   /   Circa 1916–17

American Foursquares were all the rage in the 1910s; these were two stories, squarish, with a hipped roof and one or more dormers. The house at 1110 Elm is a one-story version of a Foursquare—that is, a bungalow with a hipped roof. A simple hipped roof covers the entire structure; indeed, the roof projects forward to cover the front porch, which stretches all the way across the house. There are two front doors, which does not mean that it was originally a duplex; rather, it means that it had two front rooms and no central passage. (This was often the plan in two-story Foursquares, where the single entrance was into a living hall that incorporated the stairs.) The slight kick-out on the left side, facing west and the Paul Quinn campus, was usually where the dining room was placed in a Foursquare or in a bungalow. On the front slope of the roof was the only dormer, which had its own hipped roof matching the main roof.

This was a rent house from the start. The earliest occupants were an African American couple, J. Michael Buford and his wife, Clara. Michael was a laborer for the Exporters & Traders Compress & Warehouse Company, which was nearby at Taylor and Peach Streets. In addition to keeping house, Clara was a dressmaker. By 1921 the renters were Mitchell and Alberta Fair. Mitchell was a porter (or janitor) at the McLendon Hardware Company, and Alberta was a "hair culturist"—that is, she had a beauty shop in their house, and she was associated with Madame C. J. Walker, who became a wealthy businesswoman in the Northeast by addressing the beauty needs of middle-class African American women. As occurred with other rent houses in the neighborhood, most tenants did not stay long. Two years later Mitchell and Alberta had moved to the house next door at 1112 Elm, and 1110 Elm was occupied by two married couples: Charles and Lucille Hawkins and Lemon and May Allen. Charles was a helper at Geisler Plumbing; the occupations of the others are unclear.

Though this house seems to have a generous side lawn to the west, this was actually a separate lot. A house was built on this lot around 1906 and was the home of William E. Day, who was professor of science at Paul Quinn and also steward of the dining department. At Paul Quinn, as at many schools, teachers became adept at multitasking. ■

160. Buford-Fair House

161. Thomas and Martha Primm House

3001 Maple Avenue   /   1916–17

Remarkably, this early twentieth-century house was built for a Civil War veteran. Thomas Jefferson Primm was born in 1846 in Union, Arkansas, and fought in the war as a teenager. Tom and Mattie were in Texas by 1876 and in Waco by 1880. Tom was a farmer but for many years was the tax collector for McLennan County. When this house was built, he was 70 and working in real estate, loans, and investments. Tom and Mattie had six children, but in 1920 they were living in this house with Clara (their youngest daughter), Ethel Pearce (an adopted daughter), and two African American servants: Aaron Edwards, 50, and Lillie Bell, 17, who despite her young age worked as their cook. Ten years later the family still had two servants, but they were both white.

The house is a solid and spacious American Foursquare, a smaller version of the Dean house up the street at 3101 (see 151 in this book). It had a single-bay front porch sheltering the entrance (which was later enclosed) and two side porches with second-story rooms above each. The house was built of wood, but all of the porches were supported by brick piers with an ornamental pattern in the bricks, now obscured by a later paint treatment. The centered entrance indicated a central passage, unlike the Dean house, which had two front rooms. At the back of the lot was a two-story garage (with apartment above) and, at the west, a large one-story shed. Tom estimated the value of the house at $14,000 in 1930, well below the value of a two-story house on Austin Avenue or in Castle Heights but nevertheless quite substantial. Next door, at 3015 Maple, was the house of Shapley P. Ross, the nephew of Texas governor Sul Ross, who in 1910 married Helen Primm, a daughter of Tom and Mattie. Mattie died in 1930 at age 73, and Tom in 1937, aged 90.

161. Thomas and Martha Primm House

162. Dennis and Maggie Dodson House

2125 Colcord Avenue   /   1917–18

This house was first occupied briefly by a traveling salesman, William Y. Wilson, and his wife, Elizabeth, but by 1920 they were living on South Fourth and William was working as a night watchman. Neither traveling salesmen nor night watchmen were able to afford a home of this size. From 1918 to 1949 this was the home of Dennis S. Dodson, who was credit manager at the McLendon Hardware Company. (For his place of work, see *Historic Buildings*, 44.)

Dodson was born in Clay County, northeast of Wichita Falls. Dennis married Maggie Sisk around 1902, and they settled in Weatherford, west of Fort Worth. By 1910 they had three children—Oscar, Garnett, and Joe—and Dennis was working as a department manager at a hardware store. Another daughter, Virginia, arrived in 1912. Working at the hardware store probably put Dennis in contact with the McLendon Hardware Company of Waco, which was not only a retail hardware store but also had a large wholesale business. Around 1918 Dennis took a job with McLendon and the family moved to Waco.

Not long after moving into this house, Maggie Dodson died of pneumonia brought on by the horrible influenza epidemic of 1918. In 1920 Dennis was living with his four children, along with his sister-in-law, Maude Baker, and a niece. Within a few years he married Ella Blanche "Nelle" Symes. Both sons pursued naval careers. Oscar graduated from the US Naval Academy in 1928; Joe was a midshipman in 1930. Oscar, who served in World War II and rose to the rank of rear admiral, is buried in Arlington National Cemetery. The Dodsons were longtime members of First Presbyterian Church on Austin Avenue (see *Historic Buildings*, 3). Ella died in 1949, and Dennis in 1959, having lived in this house for more than forty years.

The house was neither as wide nor as deep as the house next door at 2123, but it was two stories high. It was a sort of a compressed Foursquare, complete with a porte cochere with a room on the second floor. Like the house at 2123 it had a shingle roof (except for the metal roof of the porch), unlike the slate roofs of the houses across the street at 2122 and 2128 built less than a decade later. The Dodson house did have a one-story garage out back, which by 1950 was enlarged to two stories to accommodate an apartment, which suggests that they had a live-in servant or hoped to attract one. This had board-and-batten walls and a hipped roof. In 1930 the family estimated the value of the house as $12,000, though that declined to $8,000 ten years later. ◼

"

162. Dennis and Maggie Dodson House

163. John M. and Edwina Sturgis Davis House

2612 Colcord Avenue   /   Circa 1917–18

This house was built for John M. Davis and his wife, Edwina (Sturgis) Davis, but early in its history the house was marked by tragedy. It was built between 1917 and 1918, making it among the earliest houses in the Dean Addition.

Edwina Sturgis Davis was the daughter of Edwin A. Sturgis Jr., a longtime vice president at Provident National Bank, and Kate (McLendon) Sturgis. Her grandfather Edwin A. Sturgis Sr. was a native of Maryland, a Confederate veteran, and mayor of Waco in the years around 1880. Her grandmother Rosalie died in 1882. Between 1889 and 1893, Edwin Sr. decided to build a new house that could be inherited by his son. He hired W. W. Larmour, who designed a two-story frame Victorian house at 526 S. Fifth, facing the original Waco buildings of Baylor University. (The site of the house is now a parking lot, facing the education building of the First Baptist Church; see *Historic Buildings*, 2.) Edwin Sr. died in 1895, and Edwin Jr. and Kate inherited the house. Their children, Rosalie, Katherine, and Edwina, all grew up in the Victorian mansion. In 1900 the household also included three African American servants.

On March 31, 1917, the *Waco Semi-Weekly Tribune* announced that Edwina Sturgis had married John M. Davis in a surprise wedding at St. Paul's Episcopal Church—only members of the immediate families knew about it. A cotton buyer in partnership with Herbert L. Turner, John was the son of W. W. Davis, a native of Arkansas, and Jimmie Craik Davis, a native of Marlin. Like Edwina, he grew up in a Victorian mansion designed by W. W. Larmour at 1700 Austin Avenue (demolished). At first, they lived in the Crawford Apartments on Austin Avenue across from where the Palm Court Apartments were built (see 154 in this book and *Historic Homes*, 84). (By then Edwina's parents had moved out of the Victorian manse into an apartment in the Kyle at 1201 Franklin.) They were in this house by May 1918, when Edwina threw a luncheon for Dorothy Finlay, who was soon to be married.

The house had many features characteristic of an American bungalow. There was a complex arrangement of gables, and the rafter ends were exposed. The posts of the front porch rested on tall brick piers, which had a pronounced curve that created a low wall; this motif was repeated on the right side of the chimney on the east side wall. Entry was directly into the living room, which had a fireplace on the east wall, flanked by a window on each side. The generously scaled front porch wrapped around to the west side, stopping about halfway. Immediately behind the house was a one-story garage, which no longer exists. The only change to the exterior of the house are that the walls are no longer white, the original red bricks of the front porch have been painted a subdued beige-green color, and the porch has been extended along the rest of the west side and across the back of the house.

The couple enjoyed their life in the house for little more than a year, as John died on August 17, 1919, at age 30. In 1920 Edwina was a 23-year-old widow with a 2-year-old daughter, also named Edwina, and a 7-month-old son, John, who never met his father and namesake. After John's death Edwina's parents moved into the house on Colcord. Edwin was 54, and Kate 52. Also in the household were two African American servants: Annie Lewis, 40, and Edna Robinson, 19. Annie worked as the family's cook, while Edna served as the nurse for little Edwina and John.

Edwina's older sister, Katherine, had married a young doctor, Joe Shelton, who moved into the Sturgis manse on Fifth Street. However, he passed away at an early age, and by 1919 Katherine was a young widow living at 1730 Ross Avenue with Joe's brother, Tate, and his wife. (Tate was a Waco policeman.) Katherine worked as a salesclerk for the Merrick Medicine Company, which had its facility at 501 S. Eighth (see *Historic Buildings*, 45). However, Katherine died in October 1921 at age 28. The funeral was from Edwina's house on Colcord, officiated by W. P. Witsell, the rector of St. Paul's Episcopal Church. Edwina's other sister, Rosalee, married and moved to Tacoma, Washington. Their mother, Kate, often visited Rosalee during the hot Texas summers.

Edwina's father died in March 1928 at age 62. Her mother soon moved out, though she lived until 1933, when she died in Los Angeles, California. In 1930 Edwina was living in this house with her children. She was 33, Edwina was 12, and John was 10. She no longer had servants to help with the housework. Her daughter married Max Gregg and ended up in Wilmette, Illinois; her son never married and lived with his mother until her death in 1958 at age 62. By then they were living in the Crawford Apartments, the place where she and her husband had started their married life before moving to 2612 Colcord. ◼

163. John M. and Edwina Sturgis Davis House

164. Thomas Henry and Nannie Munnerlyn House

2123 Colcord Avenue   /   Circa 1918–19

This home started life as a rental, occupied in 1919 by a widow, Emma Womble; her adult son, Earl Womble, a traveling salesman; and his wife, Ella. The Womble family moved to Denver, Colorado, and in 1920 and 1921 the renters were Goodhue W. Smith, who sold Ford automobiles, and his wife, Beuna. They were well enough off that they could afford a live-in servant, 17-year-old Alma Haussler. By 1923 Thomas Henry Munnerlyn and his wife, Nannie, owned the house. Munnerlyn sold real estate and fire insurance—city properties were a specialty. They previously lived on the other side of town at 714 S. Fifth. At both locations the household included Nannie's parents, John and Elvira Kitchens. In 1920 Henry was 40, and Nannie 38. John was 70 and reported that he was a yard man for the railroad; Elvira was 65 and worked beside her daughter in the home.

Henry became ill and died in November 1928. Shortly thereafter Nannie's father died on January 2, 1929, aged 82. In the 1930 census, the household consisted of Nannie, 48; her mother, Elvira, 70; and her brother R. H. Kitchens, 42, who worked as a salesman for a coffee company. The household remained intact for most of the 1930s, until Elvira died in May 1939 at age 79. The census taker in 1940 found Nannie, 58, and R. H., 52, still living here. Nannie was head of the household, and R. H. was a shoe salesman.

The house showed a single gable to the front, with gables in the middle of both sides. A porch extended across the entire front, set underneath the main roof. Many windows were clustered in two and threes. In the classic bungalow manner, there was direct entry into the living room, with a fireplace on the side wall flanked by cabinets with small windows above. French doors in the back wall opened into the dining room, and behind this was the kitchen. On the west side were three bedrooms. ◼

164. Thomas Henry and Nannie Munnerlyn House

165. Louis and Ada Roter House

2700 Washington Avenue / 1920

The Roter house is an essay in the Arts and Crafts style—that is to say, a bungalow. It looks quite small from the front, but the plan was essentially a backward "C" with an open court or patio facing Twenty-Seventh Street. Kate Edmonds, the society editor of the *Waco News-Tribune*, noted that all the rooms opened onto this patio, "where birds, flowers and sunlight flourish." This outdoor room has since been enclosed, and the rear wing has been expanded to the west, which added more year-round space yet lost something of the simplicity and charm of the original house.

The house was frame with stuccoed walls, with the entrance centered and flanked on both sides by a trio of windows. There was no front porch proper, but a roof resting upon prominent brackets provided shelter to anyone going up the front steps. The green roofing may or may not be original, but it is appropriate to the style. Centered on the roof was a low shed dormer, which had louvers rather than windows, indicating that it was there to provide ventilation to the attic rather than to actual rooms.

Louis James Roter and Ada K. Roter were both native Texans but recent arrivals to Waco. They arrived in 1916 or 1917, when Louis became the vice president and manager of the Price-Booker Manufacturing Company, which processed and canned pickles. After living for a couple of years on North Eleventh Street, they were in this house by July 1920, when Ada Roter had out-of-town guests and honored them with a dance. In that year Louis was 53 and Ada was 47.

Apparently, they enjoyed foreign travel; in 1921 Ada spent two months in Mexico City and was later joined by Louis. The *Waco News-Tribune* reported that "they were very much impressed by Mexico City." That December Ada and her sister, Mrs. J. W. House, were the victims of a shocking crime. Thieves entered the house, chloroformed them both, and made off with eight diamond rings and a diamond ear bob. The diamonds were valued at some $7,000, which would be greater than $90,000 a hundred years later. Not surprisingly, this was page-one news in Waco. Around 1929 the Roters moved to Dallas, and Louis opened his own pickle factory. They lived in Dallas for the rest of their lives. ■

165. Louis and Ada Roter House

166. James and Marie Fadal House

2801 Lasker Avenue   /   1922

This was one of two side-by-side homes for a family of Syrian immigrants. Moses and Mary Fadal were in Waco by 1902 and were settled in East Waco by 1904. Moses first sold fruits and groceries on Bridge Street, but by 1906 they had opened a grocery store in a one-story building at 310 Elm Street. They lived behind the store, but around 1912 they moved a few blocks west to a one-story Victorian house at 117 Preston, now the site of a basketball court. By 1920 Moses and Mary had nine children, ranging in age from 23 to 1, which must have made the house incredibly crowded. Around 1921 Moses and sons James and Harvey opened a drugstore on the other side of the river. Moses and Mary continued to live in East Waco, but James and Harvey moved to this house, joined by Harvey's bride, Rose.

The house is a bungalow with a wooden frame enhanced with a brick veneer. As in most bungalows, there are many gables: two on the front and three on the east side. There are trios of windows on both the front and east side, and the porch wraps around to face the side street as well as Lasker. This large porch essentially created a room for outdoor living. Most bungalows were built of wood, but the use of brick here may suggest an awareness that brick cottages were becoming quite popular.

By 1930 James and his wife, Marie, had moved into a house at 3101 Colcord; and 2801 was occupied by Harvey, Rose, and their three sons, Harvey, Edmond, and Walter. Rose was a native of Oklahoma, but both her parents were from Syria. By that time Harvey and Rose also had neighbors: Harvey's parents, Moses, and Marie, plus five sons and one daughter-in-law. ■

166. James and Marie Fadal House

167. Peach Street Shotgun House

210 Peach Street   /   Circa 1924–25

The lot on which this house sits was at the boundary between industrial and residential East Waco. By the 1920s Taylor Street to the east had pretty much been filled with one-story frame houses. These were simple yet dignified homes for working-class people. This end of the block had a grocery store at the corner of Peach and Taylor, which was demolished to make way for a filling station. Two small stores, selling groceries and ice, were next door on Peach. On the opposite side was the Blue Bird Tourism Park, a stopping place for people on the move.

From the south side, this house looks to be a classic shotgun house. Three evenly spaced windows indicate three rooms of roughly equal size, arranged in a line from front to back. The three core rooms are a living room and two bedrooms. The narrow façade probably precluded windows to the side of the centered door, but evidence suggests that the front door had a transom over it, allowing afternoon light into the front room.

Two things make this a slightly more elaborate house: a porch on the north side of the house, about the depth of the front room, and two additional rooms, a bathroom under the same lean-to roof as the side porch and a kitchen under a hipped wing that projects out on the north side. While most Waco shotguns postdate the Victorian era, this house has shingles in the gable, an older-fashioned feature.

The house was a rental property for working-class white people from the beginning, and the stays were often not long. The earliest known occupants were Lewis and Pearl Midgett in 1926. Ironically, Lewis did not work in the neighborhood but across the river as a clerk at Sanger Brothers. In 1928 Ulma and Lena Norman were residing here; Ulma was a driver for the Waco Cotton Oil Mill.

In 1930, as the Great Depression was deepening, five people lived in this little house: Thomas Kirby, 51; his wife, Roxie, 49; their sons, Homer, 25, and Wayne, 21; and Wayne's wife, Ida, 23. Thomas was a laborer in a gravel pit, as were both his sons. Ida also had a job at the Waco Packing Company, buyers and packers of poultry, eggs, turkey, and pecans. Presumably, Roxie cooked all the meals, did the laundry, and cleaned the house, which the census always recorded as "occupation: none." The Kirby family paid fifteen dollars a month to rent this house. In that same year a shotgun house on the other side of the river might rent for ten to twelve dollars a month, though an expanded shotgun might rent for eighteen to twenty dollars.

In 1932 William and Lula Johnson both lived and sold ice here. And in 1934 William and Lillian Bressler were the occupants. William worked nearby as a ginner at Thomas V. Henderson's cotton gin. The longest-term early occupants were C. Henry Hodde and his wife, Caroline. From 1936 to 1939 they lived here while running a grocery store in the building between this house and the filling station. The grocery was no longer in business by 1941, and used cars were being sold there. The house was now occupied by a widow, Bee Moore. Though their stays were short, this little house provided shelter for many working-class people as they attempted to stay afloat in tumultuous economic times. ◼

167. Peach Street Shotgun House

168. First Presbyterian Manse
(Charles and Millicent Caldwell House)

313 Crescent Road   /   1925

168. First Presbyterian Manse (Charles and Millicent Caldwell House)

This house was built by the First Presbyterian Church for its pastor. The first occupant was the Reverend Charles T. Caldwell and his wife, Millicent Lupton Caldwell. A native of Bonham, Texas, he attended Southwest Presbyterian University in Clarksville, Tennessee, where he earned a bachelor's degree and a divinity degree. He returned to Texas in 1894 to serve as pastor at the First Presbyterian Church in Greenville. He was briefly co-pastor of First Presbyterian in Houston but came to Waco in 1903. At that time the church was at 818 Austin (now a parking lot), and he took furnished rooms with Mary Jurney, who rented rooms to single men in her frame two-story at 120 N. Ninth Street (also now a parking lot).

In fall 1906 he married Millicent Lupton of Leesburg, Virginia, who was the daughter of a minister and then married one. They moved into an older house at 1004 Austin, which started out as a one-story U-shaped brick house that later had a frame second story added. This was a block farther away from the church, but the location became more convenient when a new church was built at 1100 Austin (see *Historic Buildings*, 3). In between their houses and the new church was the Prather-Darden house, which later became the Compton Funeral Home. In 1916 Charles Caldwell was singled out by W. E. B. Du Bois as the only Waco minister to speak out against the horrific lynching of Jesse Washington.

In 1925, after years of faithful service, First Presbyterian gave Charles Caldwell an all-expenses-paid trip to the Holy Land. While he was gone, they built a new manse in the Karem Park Addition. It was to be two brick-veneered stories, twenty-eight by forty feet, and to cost $12,000. The final cost was $14,000, which was still quite reasonable. The contract was awarded in March 1925 to N. A. Palmer. A native of Nebraska, Norman Palmer was a recent arrival to Waco but won the contract to remodel Pat Neff's house on Austin Avenue while building this one. The day after Caldwell's return to Waco, the family moved into the house.

The house was roughly symmetrical, with a tall, hipped roof. The entry was marked by a one-story porch of Doric piers with a Colonial Revival balustrade above. There was no door or window that could provide access onto this balcony, but the space where such an opening would have been was marked by darker-colored header bricks. It did not have the standard two windows flanking the central entrance on each side. Instead, the door was flanked by one large window on each side.

The house was built without a central passage and instead had one large front room. Presumably a larger single room would be more useful when holding church-related social events. On the north side wall was a fireplace; the mantel was in the Colonial Revival style, relatively simple in its ornament but well proportioned. Flanking it were built-in bookcases with glazed doors, a more old-fashioned feature that might be found in a bungalow or Foursquare. Beyond this room on the northeast was the staircase, and in fact the stair projects out on the north side as if it were a "stair square" on an American Foursquare. On the southeast was the dining room, and to the right of this was a door leading onto an open porch, which had a second-floor screened-in sleeping porch above it. Both porches are now enclosed.

After the Caldwell family moved out of 1004 Washington, the property was sold to A. C. Patton and the old house was demolished. Soon a one-story commercial building took its place, also built by N. A. Palmer. In recent years this has become a design store called Simply Irresistible (see *Historic Buildings*, 30) ◼

169. Jesse and Emma Harrison House

1018 Taylor Street   /   Circa 1899, enlarged circa 1932

Supposedly this house was built for George Butler shortly after the Civil War. However, there is no evidence of Butler having lived on this side of the river, and, indeed, there is no evidence for this house existing before 1899. Though it is certainly not the oldest house in East Waco, the first floor was definitely in existence in 1899 and sheltered a farm family and various working-class white families until it was purchased by a black couple, Jesse and Emma Harrison, around 1932. They enlarged it and made it their own.

In 1899 Taylor Street was filling up with one-story frame houses; this house stood out for being made of brick, for being set back farther from the street than any of its neighbors (which

169. Jesse and Emma
Harrison House

suggests that this house came first), and for having angled corners in all three of its original rooms. Although a small house, it had a distinctively sculptural quality. (The angled corners can still be seen on the west side of the house.) The segmental windows (that is, window tops that are a segment of a semicircle) is characteristically Victorian, as is the use of brick for both ornamental and structural purposes. The fireplace in the northeast room was articulated on the outer east side wall, though its upper part has been removed. The only frame part of the house was the front porch at the southeast corner.

In 1900 the house was occupied by George and Ada Lane and their three children. George was a native of Missouri and a saloon keeper, while Ada was from Mississippi; all three children were born in Texas. They did not stay in Waco long enough to make it into a city directory. The next known occupant, in 1907, was Lawrence O. Hoffman, a packer for the McLendon Hardware Company. This firm shipped a lot of hardware out of Waco on the railroad that ran beside its building between Franklin and Mary Avenues (see *Historic Buildings*, 44).

Three years later the occupant was John T. Luther, who was a ginner (or machinist) at the East Waco Cotton Gin Company. He, too, was a short-term resident, soon replaced by Samuel R. Lambert and his wife, Sallie. Samuel worked for Charles N. Kent selling hand goods, then opened a furniture store with Pleasant C. Wassum. In 1930 Richard Lott, who worked at a cement plant, and his wife, Rosalie, were renting the house for ten dollars a month.

Soon thereafter a new era began for the house when Jesse and Emma Harrison purchased it. Jesse had worked for a number of years as a porter at the United Cigar Stores Company; by 1940 he was working as a packer at the Cooper Grocery Company, a prosperous Waco business that supplied groceries to mom-and-pop stores across Central Texas. Emma worked as well, serving as health supervisor for the "colored schools" in Waco. Jesse had a high school education, and Emma had two years of college. They were both native Texans.

The Harrisons added a second floor to the house, which largely shaped its current appearance. This section was frame atop the brick first floor, with a hipped roof. The rafter ends were exposed, in the manner often seen on bungalows. They placed a staircase in the northeast room, starting on the north wall and continuing on the west wall; its simple squarish balusters seem to echo the arts and crafts movement of the early twentieth century. The final change to the main house was the enclosure of the original porch with cinder-block walls covered with brick on the exterior. Jesse and Emma also added a garage with an apartment above at the northeast corner of the property, showing that they owned an auto and required more space either for family or for renters. ■

Colonial Revival

170. Peter and Eva Taylor House
(also known as the Johnson-Taylor House)

1507 N. Fifth Street   /   Circa 1912

This house was long thought to have been built "sometime between the years 1873–79" and that "basic architectural changes" were made in 1914 to make it "a house of the grand manner." It has therefore been called the Johnson-Taylor house. However, Sanford Johnson ran a meat market in the city market building, not an especially remunerative profession, and it is extremely unlikely that he started this house. He was living in town until 1880 and left Waco around 1887. The fact that the present house is set so far back from the street suggests that a smaller Victorian house stood at the front of the lot.

What is known with a high degree of certainty is that by 1907 Peter and Eva (Carter) Taylor, a couple from Owensboro, Kentucky were living at this address. Peter worked as a city salesman for the Cooper Grocery Company; given that Cooper was a wholesale grocery, that meant that Peter was the liaison with all the mom-and-pop grocery stores in town. (Those who worked with stores in outlying areas were considered traveling salesmen.) For several years they lived at 1417 S. Eleventh Street, a one-story frame Victorian cottage just north of Speight—a neighborhood now filled with apartments for students at Baylor University. By 1905 they had four children: Roy McGlasson, Lillian, William Allan, and Robert Harold. Peter was doing well enough at Cooper Grocery that they could afford a live-in servant. In 1900 this was Nannie Peal, a 24-year-old African American who worked as the family's cook. Ten years later the cook was Halda Remus, an 18-year-old who had been born in Germany.

Between 1910 and 1911 Peter left Cooper Grocery and opened his own business, Taylor-Holloway Grocery Company. Frank James was president, Peter was secretary, and Sam Hanna was treasurer, but there was also funding from out of town: the vice president was M. B. Orde of Chicago. Two years later Orde was out of the picture, and the firm was renamed the Hanna-James-Taylor Company, still dealing in wholesale groceries. They erected the building at 212–220 S. Second Street, which is still standing and has been adapted for use as loft apartments (see *Historic Buildings*, 47). By 1916 M. B. Orde was back in the picture. However, the company went out of business between 1917 and 1919. By 1919 a new company was formed and occupied the same building: the Meadows Grocery Company. In addition to wholesaling groceries, the company roasted coffee and peanuts. Peter Taylor was the sales manager, and oldest son, Roy, was a salesman.

Around 1911, after his rapid rise at Cooper Grocery, Peter and Eva decided to build a new brick house that had round-arched windows used consistently on both the first and second floors. Those for the right front room were actually French doors on both the west and south sides. The entrance had both side lights and an elliptically arched window above. The front porch had a portico of four double-height columns, which were based on the simple Corinthian order found at the Tower of the Winds in Athens. This order had been published in *The Antiquities of Athens* by James Stuart and Nicholas Revett (1762), which became a source book for the Greek Revival. Most neoclassical buildings of the early twentieth century opted for Roman rather than Greek columns—its use here suggests that a professional architect was involved, and a rather erudite one at that. On the south side was a smaller porch of only one story, with more commonplace Doric columns. While one might consider that these columns made the house Neoclassical Revival in style, the Taylors and their neighbors considered it to be Colonial. To their generation "colonial" did not mean "before 1776" but before urbanization, industrialization, and immigration. Inside the mantelpieces continued the neoclassical theme, and the elegant staircase in the hall looks as if it could have been made in the 1850s.

The house was finished by June 1913, when the *Waco Morning News* reported on a party thrown at "the handsome new home of Mrs. P. G. Taylor." In February 1915, the birthday of George Washington inspired a "Martha Washington party" for the Young Women's Auxiliary of the First Baptist Church. The *Morning News* opined that "colonial in its every detail, even to the spacious grounds, the home of Mrs. P. G. Taylor is admirably fitted to receive guests for a colonial party." A cherry tree was brought in for the occasion, flags and hatchets were used for decorative purposes, and the family's Victrola played patriotic songs. In 1926 the house was included in the *Waco Chamber of Commerce News* home and garden issue, "Beautiful Waco." Even then the trees planted on the west and south sides of the yard were beginning to obscure the house from view.

The Taylors owned the land from Fifth Street all the way over to Fourth Street, and around 1912 they built four bungalows facing east onto Fourth Street, identical in floor plan. They certainly expected that these would be income-producing properties, which would be very helpful to Eva if Peter died first, which he did. The first batch of renters, in 1913, included a clerk at M. D. Dugger & Son Grocers, bookkeepers at Sanger Brothers and Hill Printing and Stationery, and a widow. By 1917 the northernmost of the four houses, 1706, was occupied by Roy M. Taylor and his new wife, Edith Fauquet. Edith was the daughter of Amede and Ollie Fauquet, who built the house at 1106 Taylor Street in East Waco (see *Historic Homes*, 19). Both the Fauquets and Roy and Edith moved farther west: Amede and Ollie to 2020 Ethel, and Roy and Edith to 2100 Homan, only two blocks apart. Peter Taylor died in 1941 at age 71; Eva died in 1960 at age 90.

Mrs. G. H. (Nell) Pape, one of Waco's leading philanthropists, bought the house in 1957 and donated it to the Waco Council of Garden Clubs. Pape also moved the Earle-Harrison house (see *Historic Homes*, 3) to land just north of the Taylor house and had it restored. ◼

2300 Gorman Avenue   /   1920–21

This house was an excellent example of a Colonial Revival house in Waco, with five bays and a centered door. There was a porte cochere on the left; unlike other Colonial Revival houses that were to soon follow, there was no matching sunroom on the right side. The pedimented entrance was of a sort popular in eastern cities in the late eighteenth century, when the Georgian version of the Colonial style was slowly giving way to the Neoclassical. The porte cochere used both rounded columns and square piers in the Doric order; above was a railing with short piers, simple balusters, and squares with wooden balusters running horizontally, vertically, and diagonally, known as a Roman lattice. Not surprisingly, the porte cochere faced the side street. (Sometime between 2013 and 2018 the porte cochere was removed, and a pergola of unpainted

171. Elton and Maude
Hunter House

wood took its place.) The walls consisted of a brick veneer placed over a core of tile blocks; this arrangement was more fireproof than a wooden frame.

Inside, there was a central passage with the staircase attached to the left side wall. The balusters are thick and turned, more neoclassical than truly colonial. In more grandiose versions of the Colonial, such as the Shear-Callan house or the Lee B. and Estelle Standefer Smyth house at 2211 Colcord, the staircase was freestanding in the center of the room (for the latter, see *Historic Homes*, 62). The living room was to the left, and the dining room to the right. In the living room the fireplace was on the side wall, and to the right of this was a pair of French doors that opened onto the porte cochere. The mantelpiece was strongly neoclassical, featuring engaged and fluted Doric columns, a central motif of a basket of fruit (typical of the Federal era on the East Coast), and a torch above each column. On the right side were the dining room, a small breakfast nook, and the kitchen. The room behind the living room had large sliding-glass doors on the side and the back, which are clearly not original: this space was originally an open porch. In the back was a two-story outbuilding, a garage on the first floor and an apartment above.

The original owners were Elton P. Hunter and his wife, Maude. Elton was the general manager of the William Cameron Lumber Company, an important Waco business that had been around since the 1870s. Within a few years Elton and his house were featured in a book about the firm, *A History of Wm. Cameron & Co., Inc.*, as was treasurer L. D. Dewey and his bungalow on Austin Avenue (see *Historic Homes*, 48). Dewey's house was one story but with considerable space under the roof; Hunter's was a full two stories.

When they built this house, Elton was 38 and Maude 34. They were both native Texans. Elton had four years of college under his belt, and Maude was a high school graduate. In 1930 they had a live-in maid, Clara Werner, a German immigrant who preferred to speak in her native language. In the years around 1930, she could have conversed with the Hunters' neighbor, Herbert C. Hafer, proprietor of Hafer's New Temple Drug Store (see *Historic Buildings*, 86), who also was more comfortable speaking German. In 1940 the occupant of the garage apartment was Frances Retchek, a single white female with a second-grade education; she worked as the housekeeper and paid the Hunters twelve dollars a month in rent. (In 1940 the Joseph M. Dawson family was paying fifty-five dollars to rent the entire house next door.) The Hunters estimated the value of their house at $25,000 in 1930, but this had dropped to $10,000 by 1940. ◼

172. Williamson-Eastland-Woodson House

2525 Austin Avenue / Circa 1920–21

This house may well be the earliest "Southern Colonial" style house in Waco. It predates the Ralph and Betty McLendon house at 2920 Austin Avenue by five years or so. Southern Colonial homes tend to have a portico across the entire front with two-story columns as well. This, of course, was not Colonial at all but Greek Revival, which was popular in the 1820s and beyond; for Americans in the 1920s, anything predating the Victorian was "Colonial" and thus in good taste. However, this house has columns in the Composite order—that is, a blending of Ionic and Corinthian into an even more elaborate order—which was, in fact, Roman rather than Greek. The ornate entrance has side lights but also an elliptical fanlight above, which was found not in the Greek Revival but in the earlier Federal style.

This would not bother clients desiring a Colonial Revival style; in fact, it probably would not have bothered Abner Cook, the master builder responsible for the Texas Governor's Mansion, had he been able to find craftsmen who could make Composite capitals. More disturbing to Cook and other Greek Revivalists would be the use of only four columns on a five-bay façade. Four columns would not line up with the door and the two windows of each front room; the columns did not respect the symmetry of the front wall.

When this house was put up for sale just a few years after it was completed, it was described as "containing eight rooms, two baths, large hall, sleeping porch, hardwood floors throughout, hot water heating plant, garage and all necessary outbuildings." Just a few years later an article in the *Waco News-Tribune* praised the house as "beautiful in its colonial simplicity."

The house was built for James D. Williamson and his wife, May. James was born in Texas, and May in Georgia; in 1920 he was a lawyer in private practice, with an office in the Provident Building, the great Victorian business block at Fourth and Franklin (now a parking lot). In 1919 they were living at 1626 Washington Avenue; by 1921 they were in this house. In October of that year they were advertising for a cook—"none but experienced need apply." By October 1924 they were seeking a buyer for the house. Apparently they found one, for another advertisement on January 1, 1925, offered furniture and bric-a-brac "for quick sale." Soon James and May were living in St. Louis, and James was practicing law there.

By September 1927 the house was occupied by Dr. Doyle L. Eastland and his wife, Margaret Thomas Eastland. Doyle was born in Salado, came to Waco to study at Baylor, then pursued his medical studies at the University of Pennsylvania. He served in World War I as a surgeon, rising to the rank of major. In 1920 Doyle was living with his widowed father and three younger siblings at 1226 N. Eighteenth Street. This was close to the Providence Sanitarium, where he was working.

By the fall of 1927 Doyle and Margaret were in this house. In that month Margaret's father, Cullen F. Thomas, visited them. Cullen had studied law at the University of Texas and opened a law office in Waco with William L. Prather, who later became president of UT. Thomas had represented Waco in the state legislature in 1895–96 and also served as McLennan County attorney.

Meanwhile, Dr. Doyle Eastland had become a popular Waco physician, specializing in diseases of the eye, ear, and nose. His office was on the twelfth floor of the Amicable (ALICO) Building.

  Chapter Three

Sadly, in January 1929 he caught influenza while treating patients; this developed into pneumonia. He passed away on January 12 at age 45. Margaret, 33, was still living here in 1930, but her only companion was her grandmother, Margaret R. Moore, who was 78. By 1934 the house was occupied by W. W. Woodson and his wife, Mary. ■

172. Williamson-Eastland-Woodson House

173. William and Mary Darden House

2424 Austin Avenue   /   Circa 1922

This was a low-key house for a power couple, in that respect similar to the Rotan house across the street. William Edward Darden was a native of North Carolina and attended the University of North Carolina. He had a lumber, builder's hardware, and paint store on Elm Avenue in East Waco. Mary L. Prather Darden was a native of Waco; her father, William Lambdin Prather, was a Waco lawyer who served as the president of the University of Texas from 1899 until his death in 1905. He was fond of reminding the students that "the eyes of Texas are upon you," which eventually became the inspiration for the school song.

Mary grew up in the Prather house on Austin Avenue, across Eleventh Street from the First Presbyterian Church; after her marriage to William Darden, he moved into the house as well. After the Dardens moved uptown, the old house became the Compton Funeral Home. At the time of the Waco tornado in 1953 so many had died that they had to be laid out on the sidewalk

173. William and Mary
Darden House

along Eleventh Street while awaiting burial. The house was eventually demolished and replaced with a midcentury-modern motel, which in turn has been demolished.

The new Darden house blended Arts and Crafts with Colonial Revival. The frame house had a brick veneer; the hipped roof projected well past the walls; the windows of the front rooms were in trios, an unmistakably modern touch. The centered one-story front porch had square piers, which spoke of the Arts and Crafts; the porch on the left side, which had a sleeping porch above, featured two-story brick piers at the corners, but one-story piers with classical-looking capitals in between. On the rear elevation was a porte cochere, again with a room above. On the roof were three dormers, both front and back, with segmental (i.e., a segment of a semicircle) tops. At the back of the lot was a two-story garage with doors for two cars.

The house was sufficiently impressive to make the *Waco Chamber of Commerce News* issue on "Beautiful Waco" in 1926—on the same page with the Rotan house across the street at 2425 and the Staton house one block up at 2524. When former secretary of the navy Josephus Daniels spoke at Baylor in April 1924, he stayed with the Dardens, who hosted an "informal dinner" in his honor. In fact, W. E. Darden and A. J. Armstrong, chair of the English Department, showed Daniels the Browning room in Carroll Library, which Daniels found very impressive. In his speech he blasted the Republican Party for the Teapot Dome scandal, which he characterized as "a perfect malaria of dishonesty."

Mary Darden was a member of the Woman's Club, which had been founded in 1892; its members included Kate Rotan, Jennie Dossett, Yvonne Duncan, Flora Cameron, and Louise Earle. Waiting in the wings was a "substitute member," Pauline Brazelton, who was then living at 2800 Morrow but would soon move into the Rotan house on Austin. When William Darden died in 1932 at age 64, Mary announced that she would become president of the lumber company. She continued to live in the house until her death in 1946. ■

174. J. Luther and Mae Staton House
(Staton-Dumas House)

2524 Austin Avenue / 1922–23

Architect Birch D. Easterwood, in looking back over eight years of architectural practice in Waco, declared this house to be an "Easterwood Landmark." Built on a prominent corner lot at an elevated spot on Austin Avenue, the house was more studiously Colonial Revival than many other Easterwood houses. All the windows were evenly spaced, avoiding the double or triple windows often found in houses of the 1920s. There were sunrooms on both ends (though the one on the east was originally an open porch), and there was a chimney on both end gables. The ornate entrance was in a late-Georgian style. The simple pitched roof had three dormers. Like many houses on this stretch of Austin Avenue, it was included in the *Waco Chamber of Commerce News* "Home and Garden" issue in 1926.

The original owners were James Luther Staton and Ina Mae (Sebastian) Staton. Both Luther and Ina grew up in Moody, at the southwestern corner of McLennan County. They moved to Waco in the 1910s, and Luther opened a business selling land and offering loans to buyers. While living in a bungalow at 1912 Mitchell, they had a son, James L. Staton Jr. In 1920 they owned their home and could afford a live-in maid, Hattie Miles.

The contract to build the house was awarded to Callan and Skipworth in August 1922. (James V. Callan and L. A. Skipworth were briefly partners in the early 1920s.) The house was to cost $25,000. The family was in its new house on Austin Avenue by June 1923. However, in December 1924 James Luther Staton died at age 43 after a prolonged illness. He died in the house, as was typical of the time, and the burial was from the house as well, officiated by the Reverend R. G. Bowers of Columbus Avenue Baptist Church. James was buried at Oakwood Cemetery, and the family ordered a large gray granite monument with an angel carved of white marble.

Ina was now a 28-year-old widow. Like Mary Darden one block down, she decided to continue her husband's business and was still working at it in 1930. She used her grand house as the setting for many events surrounding the wedding of her younger sister, Lula Lee Sebastian, to Burney Shook. The wedding took place at Columbus Avenue Baptist, followed by a reception at the house. The couple honeymooned in Havana. The marriage lasted less than two years, and Lula reverted to her maiden name. She moved in with her sister and began to teach piano lessons. By 1930 the household consisted of Ina; her son James, 11; her sister Lula; and her mother, who, like Ina, was a widow. Living in the two-story garage were three African American servants: George Bookman, the cook; Ed Hurs, the chauffeur; and Will Dean, the yard man.

Ten years later the household was reduced to Ina and her son. Living in the garage apartment were Ellonia Jones, the Statons' cook, and her husband, Clifton Jones, who gave his occupation as preacher. Ina lived until 1990, dying on April 15, her ninety-fourth birthday. She then joined her husband at Oakwood. ◼

174. J. Luther and Mae Staton House (Staton-Dumas House)

175. Coleman and Stella Kendrick House

2801 Maple Avenue   /   1923–24

Coleman and Stella Kendrick were both from rural Central Texas, east-southeast of Waco. Coleman was born in 1883 and grew up on a farm near Thornton in Limestone County. In 1898, at age 16, he started working for the Wilson Brothers in their general store in Thornton. In 1904 he married Stella Wilson, either the daughter or sister of one of the Wilson Brothers. In 1919 they had a son, Joe Wilson Kendrick, and moved to the town of Mart, where Coleman opened his own store. Mart was on the county line between Limestone and McLennan Counties and was thus much closer to Waco.

Apparently, the store in Mart did very well, because Coleman and Stella began to contemplate retirement and a move to Waco. They hired architect Birch D. Easterwood to design a Colonial Revival house for them. The house was finished by 1924, when Easterwood listed it among the "Easterwood Landmarks" that he had designed in his eight years of architectural practice. Apparently, the family lived partly in Waco and partly in Mart, because Coleman did not officially retire from business until 1928. By 1940 they had a live-in servant: Ruth Horton, a 30-year-old African American, worked as their cook and lived in a small apartment attached to their one-story frame garage.

The house was a straightforward expression of the Colonial Revival style: a veneer of red brick and a careful bilateral symmetry with chimneys on both end elevations and matching porches on each side (enclosed sometime after 1950). Also characteristic of the Colonial Revival was the semicircular front porch, which had thin Doric columns that were from the slightly later neo-classical era. A feature that made it clear that this was a house of the 1920s and not the 1750s or 1790s was the use of triple windows on both the first and second floors. Such wide openings were not structurally possible in a house with load-bearing brick walls.

The house was quite similar to the Thomas and Lucy Jarman house at 3211 Austin Avenue, designed by Herman F. Cason (see *Historic Homes*, 63). This house was designed in November and December 1923 and built the next year. Where each set of windows in the Kendrick house had three equally sized windows, the Jarman house had a larger central window and narrower windows on both sides. Moreover, the Jarman house had paired windows on the second floor and three dormers on the roof. In 1930 the Kendricks estimated that their house was worth $20,000, while the Jarmans estimated theirs at $30,000.

In Waco the Kendricks were members of the Central Christian Church. Perhaps Coleman put in a good word for Easterwood with the church, because by July 1924 Easterwood was making plans for a new church building for 1100 Washington (see *Historic Buildings*, 11). Both Coleman and Stella lived in this house for the rest of their lives. Coleman died there in 1946 at age 62, and Stella died there in 1965 at age 78. Their son Joe had moved out by the time of his mother's death but had not gone far: he was living at 3100 Maple, the Chambers-Murphey-Kendrick house (see 181 in this book). That house was an even more impressive example of the Colonial Revival. ■

175. Coleman and Stella Kendrick House

176. Harry T. Cruger House

3025 Maple Avenue / 1924

This was the house of the first Ford dealer in Waco. Harry T. Cruger was born in Bell County, south of Waco; his father was from New York, and his mother was from Virginia. His father was a farmer and a stock raiser. Harry had an older brother, Frank, and younger sisters, Nettie and Fannie. The family moved to Waco in the 1870s and settled into a house at the southwest corner of Speight and South Ninth Streets. Though raised on a farm, Harry had a way with machinery and called himself a mechanical engineer or machinist. His first job was with the Ed. Stephenson Manufacturing Company, which made mattresses, bed springs, and the like, and Harry did similar work for the R. T. Dennis Manufacturing Company. Around 1903 or 1904 he moved to the Banning Machinery Company, which made or sold engines; boilers; gasoline engines; pumps; pipe; hose; fittings; rubber and leather belting; gin, mill, and threshing machinery; and windmills. Clearly many of these products were of greatest use to farmers, but by 1907 Harry was also an agent for Ford automobiles. By 1911 he was calling himself a Ford dealer with a shop at 614 Austin Avenue, where he sold autos and accessories. In 1922–23 Harry built a new garage at 922 Austin to house his business (see *Historic Buildings*, 26). By 1926 he was selling both Fords and Lincolns as well as Fordson tractors.

Harry married sometime before 1900. His wife, Helen, was born in Durham, Maine; this was her second marriage, and sometimes her unmarried daughter from the first marriage, Nettie Autrey, lived with them. In 1920 her grandson, Raymond Denton, was working for Harry as an auto salesman. Helen died in 1920 of cancer of the stomach. Perhaps Harry could not imagine

remaining in the house at 724 N. Fourteenth where they had lived for more than a decade, and he decided to build a new house.

Cruger hired the Waco architect James P. Baugh to design his new house. Baugh had worked as a draftsman for Birch D. Easterwood on such houses as the Laidlaw-McDermott house (see *Historic Homes*, 98) and had already designed the Clifford and Rebecca Swift house on Austin Avenue (see *Historic Homes*, 59). By May 1924 Baugh was working on the design of this house; in June the contract to build a two-story, brick-veneered house was awarded to Joseph F. Cason, who had been a Waco contractor for decades. The initial contract was for only $8,000, but in 1930 Harry estimated the value at $20,000, which was more in line with the value of other houses of this caliber.

Most Colonial Revival houses in Waco used a dark red brick, but the Cruger house utilized bricks of a brown color. As with most Colonial Revival houses, sets of three windows were clustered together on the first floor, and double windows were paired above. In the center was a one-bay porch with paired columns. In 1930 Harry was a 67-year-old widower living with his stepdaughter, Nettie, and an African American maid, Clara Clamance. He died in 1938. ■

176. Harry T. Cruger House

177. Valentine and Kathleen Cox House
(Nabors-Cox House)

2925 Maple Avenue / 1925

This two-story, brick-veneered residence was designed for Charles and Ella Nabors but was the longtime home of Valentine and Kathleen Cox. Charles and Ella hired Birch D. Easterwood to design their house in February 1923 with a budget of $25,000. Charles was the co-owner of Wilson, Nabors & Co., cotton exporters. (Gus Pape, the husband of Waco philanthropist Nell Pape, was a partner before forming his own business.) For some reason, construction was delayed, but the Nabors were in their house by 1925. In that year another couple, Valentine and Kathleen Cox, began conversations with Easterwood about designing their house. However, they

seem to have wanted a two-story, brick-veneered house for $11,000 or $12,000, and the project went nowhere. They ended up buying a recent Easterwood house from Charles and Ella Nabors and lived there for many years.

The house in its current state is dominated by a grand portico of paired Doric columns, but this was not shown on the Sanborn Map of 1926 or the 1950 update, suggesting that it was added after 1950. Originally, the most impressive feature on the house was the colonial door frame. Above this door was a casement window, on top of which was a cartouche with the letter "N" for Nabors. Both the porte cochere on the west side and the sunroom on the east were originally one story; presumably they were given a second story when the grand portico was added. The two-story, two-car garage and apartment, in a matching redbrick veneer, were original. Valentine Cox was born in Glen Rose, Texas, and learned the mercantile trade in Stephenville. He moved to Waco in 1922 and with his brothers purchased a store that became the R. E. Cox Dry Goods Store, which morphed into the Cox Department Store, long a fixture at Austin Avenue and Seventh Street. ■

177. Valentine and Kathleen Cox House (Nabors-Cox House)

178. John and Lucy Rowland House
(Rowland-Trice House)

1811 Colcord Avenue / 1925–26

This house was built by a farming family from North Texas and then lived in by a family whose income was derived from the insurance business; the two families were linked by marriage and by their deep Baptist faith. John W. Rowland and his wife, Lucy Mahala Oldham, were both native Texans who lived for many years in Montague County, first in Spanish Fort on the Red River, then in Nocona, where they lived for many years. By 1910 they had four children: Carl, Catherine, John W. Jr. (known as Jack), and Adrian. In the mid-1920s they left Nocona for the bright lights of Waco, perhaps because Jack was reaching college age and hoped to attend Baylor.

Although they built this house on Colcord, Jack and Lucy apparently decided that they preferred North Texas and the farming life. By 1930 they and their youngest son, Adrian, were living in Collingsworth County in the Panhandle, east of Amarillo, raising livestock. Daughter Catherine decided to say in Waco, apparently because she was engaged to Edwin Leslie Trice, who went by Jack. The couple may have met at Columbus Avenue Baptist Church or at Baylor, as they both attended college. The occupants of this house in 1930 were Jack Rowland Jr., 23; his wife of two years, Willie Belle (White) Rowland; and their 4-month-old son, also named Jack. The house was valued at $25,000, a tidy sum that was similar to house values on Austin Avenue. Jack's occupation was law student, which suggests that his parents were paying for the house.

Two years later John W. Rowland died and was buried back in Nocona. Lucy, now a widow, moved to Waco. However, Jack, Willie, and little Jack soon moved to Houston. The house was then occupied by Jack and Catherine Trice. In 1940 Jack was 39, and Catherine 35; they were living with their two sons, E. L. Jr., 10, and John Rowland Trice, 7, and with mother-in-law Lucy Rowland. Living in the garage apartment out back was the family's housekeeper, Margaret Kutscherovsky, a 20-year-old Texan who had lived in nearby Falls County as recently as 1935. In 1940 Jack, Willie, and their two sons were still living in Houston, and Jack was working as district manager for the Works Progress Administration, the New Deal program that attempted to mitigate the worst effects of the Great Depression.

Back in Waco, Jack Trice managed the Northwest National Life Insurance Company and later the Southland Life Insurance Company. Catherine, meanwhile, hosted many church events at their home. E. L. Trice Jr. graduated from Waco High in 1948 and became a petroleum engineer, living in Midland. John Rowland Trice graduated from Waco High in 1951, got a degree from Baylor, served in the navy, then returned to Baylor to get his law degree. He founded a Republican Club in Waco at a time when there were few Republicans in Texas. He supported John Tower for US Senate and Ronald Reagan for president; his own attempts at elective office were not successful, running for district attorney in 1962, attorney general in 1964, and governor of Texas in 1968. His father, Jack Trice, died in 1960, and Lucy Rowland died in 1967. Her daughter, Catherine Trice, continued to live in the house until she died in 1973. Her funeral was at Columbus Avenue Baptist, and she joined Jack in Oakwood Cemetery.

The two-story house was typical Colonial Revival of the 1920s: a brick veneer over a frame of wood, with a porte cochere on the west side and an open one-story porch on the east. A small

178. John and Lucy Rowland House (Rowland-Trice House)

porch with a pediment marked the front door. On both the first and second floors windows were clustered in threes, which was not possible in colonial houses where the brick walls were load bearing; such trios of windows were possible only in a Colonial Revival house with a brick veneer. A final colonial touch were the three dormer windows on the roof. The main roof and all the smaller porches were slate, which made the house very fireproof in the eyes of the Sanborn Fire Insurance mapmaker.

Inside, the house had a narrow central passage with staircase engaged to the left wall. The staircase had delicately turned balusters that were appropriate for the Colonial Revival. Apparently, the east front room was the living room; the fireplace with Colonial Revival mantel stood on the outer side wall between two French doors leading onto the side porch. The garage in back was aligned directly behind the porte cochere. An outer staircase attached to the east side led to the apartment on the second story.

A similar house stands just to the west at 1901 Colcord. It was built in 1929–30 as a parsonage for Columbus Avenue Baptist Church. In 1930 the Reverend Floyd Thorn; his wife, Irma; and their four young children lived there. In 1933 the occupants were the Reverend Carl E. Hereford and his wife, Eula. (Carl Hereford later led congregations in Lubbock, Corpus Christi, and Fort

Worth and served as the vice president of the Baptist General Convention in 1957.) In 1940 the occupants were the Reverend H. H. Hargrove; his wife, Theta (Plunkett) Hargrove; four children; and his mother-in-law, also named Theta. The lot was a little more than half the size of the Rowland-Trice lot, so there was no side yard to speak of. Like the Rowland-Trice house, this house was Colonial Revival in style and had a brick veneer; however, the architect opted for five individual windows rather than clusters of three. And the roof used wooden shingles, making it much less fireproof. There was a garage near the alley, but it was only one story and did not have an apartment. ◼

179. Charles Samuel and Regina Appell House

909 N. Eighteenth Street / 1925–26

This is an excellent example of a Colonial Revival house. It could have been designed by any number of Waco architects, including Milton W. Scott, Birch D. Easterwood, James P. Baugh, or Herman F. Cason, but this one is documented as having been designed by E. McIver Ross. Having worked as a draftsman for Scott, Ross partnered with a fellow draftsman, Herman Cason, for several years, and they designed the Texas Telephone Company Exchange, built 1915–16 (see *Historic Buildings*, 49). They later went their separate ways, and when business was slow, Ross would work for Milton Scott. The blueprints of the Penland house near Cameron Park, produced by the Milton W. Scott Company, are signed only "R," which certainly stands for "Ross." That house was completed in 1925, and Ross may have used the house to impress potential clients (see

179. Charles Samuel and Regina Appell House

Historic Homes, 60). However, Charles S. Appell was also involved in the Waco Drug Company, and Ross had dramatically enlarged its building in 1922–23 (see *Historic Buildings*, 52). Ross was at work on plans for the Appell house in the fall of 1925, and in October 1925 it was announced that five contractors had bid on the house. J. V. Callan got the contract for $18,334.

The clients were Charles Samuel Appell and Regina Marie (Flanigan) Appell. In 1925 C. S. was 41, and Regina 36. He was a native of Texas (his father was born in Baltimore, and his mother in Galveston), but she hailed from Missouri. The family was Roman Catholic. Charles was an officer of the Waco Loan & Trust Company, but he was also involved in other ventures: the Brazos Valley Cotton Oil Mill (see *Historic Buildings*, 46), the Appell-Ponder Motor Company, the Lone Star Rubber Company, and, as noted, the Waco Drug Company (see *Historic Buildings*, 52). Their first son, Charles Jr., was 6 and a half when they moved into the house, and two more children arrived later, Melbourne and Marie. In 1920 and 1930 their household also included a female servant: in 1920 Belle Miles, 21, an African American, was nurse to little Charles Jr.; in 1930 a white woman, Amanda Touchstone, 33, was working as the family cook. In 1930 the value of the house was estimated at $28,000, well above the contracted price from five years earlier.

The exuberance that may have inspired that estimate was wiped away by the Great Depression. In 1940 the family had sold the house and moved to 823 N. Seventeenth Street (no longer standing). The family was renting their new house for thirty-five dollars a month. Charles was no longer a vice president or secretary but a salesman working in real estate and loans. Charles Jr. was also working, as an agent for an insurance company. Melbourne was only 14 and not ready for the job market. However, Marie, 19, had married Everett M. McCracken, 21, who was working as an order clerk at a local lumberyard. And the family was now joined by a granddaughter, Jerre, 7 months old. Both Charles Jr. and Melbourne attended Baylor University and became prominent Waco businessmen: Charles in commercial real estate and Melbourne at Pioneer Savings Association (see *Historic Buildings*, 41).

The house had a veneer of red brick over a wooden frame. A porch stretched across the front facing Blair, though there is also a nicely articulated door at the northwest corner, facing Eighteenth Street. At the opposite end was a projection with an open porte cochere, with open sleeping porch above, now enclosed. In the rear the roof extended to a point somewhere between the first and second floors. The lean-to continued on the eastern two-thirds to create additional space. A porch ran across the southern façade, though the columns seem to have been updated. At the northeast corner of the property was a two-story garage apartment with an external staircase on the east side wall. Though the footprint of the main house is unchanged, all windows have been replaced and the dormer windows front and back rebuilt in a loose approximation of their original appearance.

Though the street address is on North Eighteenth, the house actually faces Blair. Just across Eighteenth was the Foursquare of the widow Mettie Fisher, and just across Blair was the Mission-style house of Joe and Rose Snaman. ■

180. Hafer-Dawson House

2316 Gorman Avenue / Circa 1926

Smaller than the house next door at 2300 Gorman (see 171 in this book), and with a brick veneer over a wooden frame rather than brick over tile blocks as at 2300, this house was built for a prosperous shopkeeper and his wife. While 2300 was a five-bay Colonial Revival, this was the three-bay version of the same style. The entrance hall was on the left, with formal rooms opening to the right. Even though it was only three bays, it still had a porte cochere on the left and a one-story wing on the right, though the wing was covered with wood. The value of the house was estimated at $25,000, which was comparable to that of many two-story, five-bay houses of the same era.

180. Hafer-Dawson House

The house was built for Herbert C. and Blanche Hafer. Herbert was an emigrant from Germany and still preferred to speak in his native language; Blanche was born in Louisiana, but both of her parents were from Alabama, so she had roots in the Deep South. When they built the house, Herbert was 48 and Blanche was 45; they had been married for more than two decades. Herbert was the proprietor of the New Temple Drugstore, which was the anchor tenant on the first floor of the Masonic Temple at 724 Washington Avenue. Milton W. Scott had designed this impressive headquarters for the local Masonic chapter in 1913 (see *Historic Buildings*, 86).

Herbert Hafer died around 1931, and Blanche was listed as a widow in the 1932 city directory. She had moved out by 1934, when the house was rented to Michael and Annie Yates. Michael was the manager of the Western Grocery Company. By 1936 the occupants were Thomas and Margaret Westbrook; Thomas gave his occupation as farmer in the city directories.

By 1939 the renters were Joseph and Willie Dawson. The Reverend Joseph Martin Dawson was the pastor of the First Baptist Church in Waco from 1915 to 1946 (see *Historic Buildings*, 2). At the time of the 1940 US Census, Joseph was 60 and Willie was 51. Also living with them was Joseph's dad, Martin J. Dawson, who was 83, and Willie's sister, Donna Booch, who was a 65-year-old widow. Also in the household was Mattie White, a widowed 41-year-old African American who worked as the housekeeper. Reverend Dawson was the only person in the household with a college education. In 1940 they were paying fifty-five dollars a month to rent this house. (For the home of Waco's longtime Presbyterian minister, which was actually owned by his church, see 168 in this book.) ■

181. Chambers-Murphey-Kendrick house

3100 Maple Avenue   /   1931–32

This fine Colonial Revival house was designed in the fall of 1931, and the contract to build it was awarded to J. V. Callan in October of that year. Callan had built the Alexander home at 122 Oriental and the Appell house at 909 N. Eighteenth, both designed by E. McIver Ross, which might make Ross seem a likely designer of this house. However, the clients attended St. John's Methodist Church, where they would have known the architect Herman F. Cason, who attended the church and designed its building. And, in fact, Callan had been the contractor for the Winchell house at 3003 Novice Road, which was designed by Cason (see *Historic Homes*, 106).

    The house had a simple pitched roof above brick-veneered walls. In true Colonial Revival fashion, the house had five bays—two windows to each side of the entrance—though in this case the center bay was emphasized emphatically. The entrance with an elliptical fanlight and side lights was recessed; to each side were two-story pilasters supporting a triangular pediment that was open at the bottom. All four first-story windows were topped with cast-concrete ornaments.

181. Chambers-Murphey-Kendrick House

There were chimneys at both ends, although the only fireplace was at the east end. The chimney at the west was there simply for the sake of symmetry. Above each bay was a dormer window with a round-arched top. Although the windows on the front were all separate, in true colonial fashion, on the west side wall the windows on the second floor were paired.

Inside, the entry hall was shallow, but the staircase that began on the left side made a considerable statement as it rose against the back wall of the room. To the left was the living room, with the fireplace on the east (left) side wall; to each side French doors led to a space that was originally open but was later enclosed by the Murphey family. To the right of the entrance was the dining room, behind which were the pantry and the kitchen. Behind the stair hall were the breakfast room and another sitting room that extended into the backyard by means of a half-octagonal projection. Above were four bedrooms; in between were two bathrooms, one at the front and another at the rear that shared the space with another small sitting room.

The clients were Joseph E. Chambers and Mary (Hicks) Chambers. Joseph was the proprietor of a company that sold school furnishings and supplies. In 1930 Joseph was 52, and Mary 44; they were living in Provident Heights at 2300 Parrott with their 3-year-old-son, Joseph Jr. They were in this house early in 1932. Alas, the family enjoyed this house for little more than a year, as Joseph Chambers died on June 23, 1933. Mary decided to move to a much smaller house, and by 1936 she and Joseph Jr. had moved into a house at 2400 Parrott, one block west of their earlier home. When World War II broke out, young Joseph was determined to fight and in 1943 joined the US Marines. He also served in Korea and in Vietnam before he retired in 1970. In his career he earned nineteen battle stars, a Bronze Star, and six Purple Hearts. He died in 1973 at the relatively young age of 48, but his mother continued to live on Parrott until her death in 1974 at age 89.

The new owners of 3100 Maple were Dr. Paul Chesley and Cora (Tilley) Murphey. They had previously lived at 2411 Parrott, so they virtually swapped neighborhoods with Mary Chambers. This was a late–Queen Anne house with a wrap-around porch, which burned around 2002. Paul was a surgeon who operated his own clinic. In 1940 he was 51, and Cora 50; they were both Texas natives and had college degrees. In that year their daughter, Dorothy, was 16 and a senior at Waco High. Also living with them was their maid, Elda Richter, a 25-year-old woman who was born in Texas to a father who was a native of Germany and a mother born in Texas.

Dorothy Murphey went on to get a degree in teaching and art from Baylor University. Just after World War II she married Joe W. Kendrick, who had grown up down the block at 2801 Maple (see 175 in this book). By 1954 they had two sons, Joe Jr., 7, and Chesley, 4, and a daughter Carolyn, 10 months. At first, they lived at 4020 Hubby Avenue, but they later moved into Dorothy's old home. Dorothy briefly taught art at West Junior High before her marriage but afterward taught painting classes at Art Center Waco. Joe and Dorothy were founding members of Lakewood Christian Church (Disciples of Christ) in 1957. ■

182. Carl and Elsie Wallerstedt House

201 N. Thirty-Eighth Street   /   1933

This is the house that cement built. Consisting of a brick veneer over cement walls, it was built
for Carl A. Wallerstedt, the manager of the Universal-Atlas Cement Plant in Waco. Carl was born
in Lindsborg, McPherson County, Kansas, to Gustaf Adolph and Emilia Wallerstedt, who were
Swedish immigrants. This was a farming community; however, Gustaf was not a farmer but the
superintendent of a flour mill, a service for which farmers were doubtless grateful. Young Carl
went off to see the wider world: he attended the Kansas State Agricultural College (now Kansas
State University), majoring in engineering.

After he graduated in 1917, he worked in New York City and Washington, D.C., then was
hired by the Atlas Portland Cement Company in Northampton, Pennsylvania (near Allentown),
in 1919. While living in Allentown, he met his future wife, Elise. Soon after they married, Carl
was transferred to the office in New York City, and the newlyweds moved to East Orange, New
Jersey, where their daughter, Elsie Louise, was born. In 1928 Wallerstedt was sent to Waco to

182. Carl and Elsie
Wallerstedt House

build a cement plant there. Shortly after the plant was completed, Atlas was purchased by the Universal Cement Portland Steel Company (a subdivision of US Steel) and the company became the Universal Atlas Cement Company.

At first the family lived in rent houses, but they acquired a lot at the corner of North Thirty-Eighth Street and Chateau Avenue in Castle Heights. Immediately across Chateau was the house of Ike and Katie Kestner, designed by Birch Easterwood and built in 1931 (see *Historic Homes*, 110). The Wallerstedts hired Easterwood to design their house; he was assisted by his longtime draftsman James K. Dillard and by his son, Kenneth V. Easterwood, who would soon become his partner. The blueprints were drawn up in July 1933.

This end of Castle Heights was just being developed in the early 1930s. Much as Easterwood had done on the Laidlaw-McDermott house on Colcord Avenue (see *Historic Homes*, 98), the Wallerstedt house had two principal elevations, a main entrance on Thirty-Eighth Street and a side porch facing Chateau. The house was a study in the Colonial Revival style, with thin Ionic columns framing the main entrance and equally thin Doric columns used on the side porch. The red brick and white trim were characteristic of the Colonial Revival; as on most of his Waco houses Easterwood employed modish "tapestry" bricks, which were striated to give them a rougher texture.

Though the house seems quite symmetrical from the main streets, it did have a one-story room projecting on the east side. On a more typical house this would be in the backyard (as it was on the Wolfe house on Austin Avenue; see *Historic Homes*, 112), but because of the unusual orientation of the house it is visible from Chateau. Extending north from this room was an arcaded porch, which is nearest to the garage at the northeast corner of the property. On the blueprints Easterwood depicted an arcade resting on brick piers connecting the house to the garage but requested that prospective contractors submit an alternative bid with the arcade omitted, an option that the Wallerstedts chose. The story-and-a-half, brick-veneered, two-car garage had an apartment on its upper level.

The main entrance was on Thirty-Eighth Street, which led into a fairly standard entrance hall with staircase. To the right was the living room, which stretched the entire depth of the house. The focal point of the living room was the mantelpiece, with a neoclassical basket of flowers; to each side of the fireplace was a pair of French doors leading onto the porch that faces Chateau. (In this regard the house was different from the Laidlaw-McDermott house, where doors from both the living room and dining room opened onto the porch.) On the left (north) side of the house were the dining room and the kitchen; straight ahead were the breakfast room and a powder room with sink and toilet. On the first floor all rooms had floors covered with oak, except for the kitchen, which was pine.

Upstairs were three bedrooms. The master was above the dining room and kitchen, and two smaller bedrooms were above the living room. The master bedroom was large but did not run the entire depth of the house; at the rear were a sewing room and two closets. The only bathroom was above the front part of the entrance hall. Apparently Elsie Wallerstedt enjoyed listening to the radio, as an antenna was built into the house with radio outlets in the kitchen and sewing room. In addition, there were telephone outlets in the kitchen and master bedroom. The house also had a basement under the dining room and kitchen, which was relatively rare for Waco.

In 1940 the family had expanded to four, with the addition of Carl Jr. This was a well-educated family: Carl Sr. had attended college for four years, and Elsie, for one. Elsie Louise (she ended up going by just Louise) had completed seventh grade. The family attended Central Presbyterian Church; both Carl and Elsie held many leadership positions in the church. Even after ten years of Depression the family could still afford a live-in servant. Lenore Rickey was an African American woman and a widow at 26. (Widowhood or divorce often pushed women to become live-in servants.) She was paying four dollars a month for her rooms over the garage. Elsie told the census enumerator that the house was worth $12,000; that was comparable to the Kestner house at $12,500. The drop in the Kestner house value from $18,000 was quite typical in Depression-era Waco. ■

183. Washington Terrace Apartments

1615 Washington Avenue / 1928–29

The Palm Court Apartments at 2005 Austin Avenue (see *Historic Homes*, 84) had proven to be a success, so Abe Levy of Waco decided to try a similar development. He hired a local contractor, G. C. Goodgion, to design and build these apartments in October 1928. The project was completed in just twelve weeks. Helping speed the project along was the fact that many of the materials were provided by the William Cameron Lumber Company in Waco. Ener Nelson, a Norwegian immigrant who founded his own company producing doors, window sashes, and other items, provided all the millwork, including the windows; also involved were the Waco Art Glass Company, Central Texas Iron Works, and the Waco Art Stone Company. Furnishings were from R. T. Dennis & Co. Abe Levy announced that he would require a lease of at least six months and that potential renters would be required to furnish "the best of references"—both ways of suggesting that this was a "high-class" establishment.

Stylistically the building blended the Neoclassical style with the Spanish Colonial Revival. The entrance was framed by a pair of Ionic columns, which were made locally by the Waco Art Stone Company. The two urns, almost absurdly large, were added after the original iron railing from the Central Texas Iron Works was removed. The window above was framed by an elliptical arch, which had been popular in the later part of the Federal era—between 1800 and 1820. The Washington Avenue façade had a curvilinear parapet in the middle of which was the famous Alamo motif, the only suggestion of the Spanish Colonial Revival style on the building. The exterior was a veneer of buff-colored brick over a wooden frame. Most windows were in trios or pairs—unfortunately, the original windows were all subsequently replaced. The two wrought-iron lampposts are original, though they once had "rich brown lamps."

The two-story building had sixteen apartments, and behind this was a garage that could hold twelve automobiles. Attached to the garage at the east end was a two-story apartment for the porter. In 1930 renters paid between fifty-five and eighty dollars a month. It is unclear why there was such a difference; at the Palm Court everyone was paying sixty-five dollars a month. After ten years of the Great Depression renters paid between thirty and forty-five dollars. Doubtless this was not an act of charity by the owner but based on what renters were able to pay. In 1930 most renters were in their twenties or thirties and probably hoped to buy a house as soon as the Depression was over.

The ritziest renters were Simon and Sallie Goldstein, who were 75 and 71, respectively. Simon was born in Warsaw, Poland, and Sallie was born in San Marcos, Texas. The younger sister of Isaac Goldstein, of the Goldstein-Migel Department Store, Sallie found an unrelated Goldstein to marry. Simon and Sallie actually rented two apartments for $155. The household included their daughter, Birdie; her husband, Henry Michelson, who was a salesman at a certain store in town; and their live-in servant, John B. Washington, a 44-year-old African American. Washington was most likely living beside the garage; in 1939, after both Simon and Sallie had passed away, he was still living there and working as the porter.

Other renters were young professionals: Dr. Ronald E. Cogswell and his wife, Grace, who was a schoolteacher; Sterling E. McCullough, a civil engineer; and Benjamin Pittman, who managed

183. Washington Terrace Apartments

an insurance company. Several renters were salesmen—for example, Rowe L. Sams sold furniture, and John Saunders sold automobile seat covers. Geraldine Saunders, his wife, was a secretary at a local college, presumably Baylor.

In 1939 the only holdovers were Henry and Birdie Michelson and the porter John B. Washington. (Simon had passed away in 1931, and Sallie in 1936.) Henry had been promoted at Goldstein-Migel and was now a floor manager. Other apartments housed a lawyer, E. Stansell Bryan, and his wife, Ruby, and various salesmen. May Missner was a nurse at the Veterans Administration Hospital, which had only recently opened (see *Historic Buildings*, 69; for nurses' quarters at the hospital, see 194 in this book). Two apartments were rented by single women: Mamie Schaper, a public schoolteacher, and Beatrice Merritt, a social worker. Four apartments were vacant in 1939. In 1940 two new residents were Dr. C. T. Waters, who worked at the Veterans Hospital, and his wife, Ruth, who was a secretary in the state service office for veterans. ◾

184. Charles and Clothilde Eubank House

3525 Carondolet Boulevard   /   Circa 1937–38

The Eubank house, an essay in the Southern Colonial style, was built in the years between the publication of Margaret Mitchell's novel *Gone with the Wind* in 1936 and the premiere of the movie adaptation in 1939. Houses with two-story porticoes, while not common, had been built in Waco for more than two decades, including the Ralph and Betty McLendon house at 2920 Austin Avenue, 1925–26, and the Burt and Anne Scott house at 3315 Austin, circa 1928 (see *Historic Homes*, 69 and 70). Well before either of those houses, the Alexander P. Duncan house at 1600 Austin Avenue, built circa 1907–08, was explicitly called Southern Colonial.

This latter-day Southern Colonial was built for Charles and Clothilde Eubank. Both Charles and Clothilde were Texas natives and had some college education: Charles four years, and Clothilde two. Charles was a partner in a banking and investment house with F. Glassell Elliott. Charles and Clothilde were in their late thirties when they built this house, and they had one daughter, Alice, who was in her teens. In 1940 Clothilde estimated the value of the house at $12,500, which was probably a little low.

The house was five bays with a door in the center, as was typical in colonial houses of the eighteenth century. The feature that made it *Southern* Colonial was the colonnade, even though Greek Revival houses north, south, and west had such colonnades. In this case the colonnade had just four columns, the bare minimum for Southern Colonial. Originally the columns were square piers, sometimes known as "box" columns; these were later replaced with rounded columns, the sides of which were straight up and down rather than with a gentle swell in the middle, as was expected in Greek and Greek Revival columns. The door frame is more canonical Greek Revival, with rectangular side lights and transom. The house has not been linked to any architect; it was probably designed by one of Waco's many contractors, a trend that would become more common after World War II. ■

184. Charles and Clothilde Eubank House

185. T. Walter and Eula Harrell House

3625 Castle Avenue / 1938–39

This house was apparently built as a speculative venture, and after its completion an open house was held on February 3, 4, and 5, 1939. The announcement of the open house in the newspaper makes this a well-documented example of a Southern Colonial house. Even the stylistic term "Southern Colonial" was used in the headline, just in case passersby did not catch the allusion to George Washington's Mount Vernon and to innumerable Mount Vernon knock-offs.

At exactly the same time the façade of a very similar Southern Colonial house was being built on the studio lot of Selznick International in Los Angeles for Tara in *Gone with the Wind*. The relationship between this house and Tara is entirely coincidental—principal photography on the movie started just as this house was being completed—but both movie and house are testaments to the mythic power of the Southern Colonial style.

The advertisement for the open house specified both the architect and the contractors. The architect was Herman F. Cason, who had designed the Austin Avenue houses of newspaper publisher Ephraim Fentress and his wife, Edith, and Thomas and Lucy Jarman (see *Historic Homes*, 65 and 63). (Perhaps a more relevant prototype was the Ralph and Betty McLendon house, which was the most notable Southern Colonial statement of Birch D. Easterwood; see *Historic Homes*, 69.) Around this same time Cason designed the Elite Café on Waco's Circle for the Colias Brothers (see *Historic Buildings*, 39). The contractors for the Harrell house were McClellan-Brown-McClellan, led by 34-year-old Roy C. McClellan.

The ad proclaimed, "This handsome home is of the southern colonial type, authentic in every detail of architecture. Imposingly situated atop a knoll it is strikingly identical to the homes of cherished tradition." The latter point was an allusion to Mount Vernon, the colonnade of which looked down into the Potomac River valley. The ad further emphasized that interior features such as the mantels, oak flooring, and wallpaper all alluded to the colonial period.

Though the style was colonial, the method of production was thoroughly modern. The contractors used "IDEAL mill work and fixtures" throughout the house. These included the door frame, which was a "Stockbridge" pattern, colonial panel doors, and outside ornamental blinds. All of these were factory-made and available from Cameron's Building Material Store at 901 Elm Street (now the site of the East Waco Library). The house also had a variety of wallpapers, chosen to relate to the function of the room. Minnesota paints were used inside and out. Both paints and papers could be purchased at Cameron's Wall Paper & Paint Store at 622 Austin Avenue (see *Historic Buildings*, 22).

The first owners of the house were both from rural areas south of Waco. Thomas Walter Harrell was born at Jones Prairie, ten miles northwest of Cameron in Milam County. Eula Lucille Arnett was born in Wheelock in Robertson County. They were married in Milam County and moved to Waco soon after, around 1920. Earlier Thomas was an assistant district manager at a laundry, but by 1940 he was district manager for the William Cameron Lumber Company. (For other homes of Cameron employees, see *Historic Homes*, 48; and 171 and 189 in this book.) In 1940 the census taker found them in their new home. Thomas was 45, and Eula 44. They had two

sons: Hugh, 15, and Glenn, 12. The family attended Columbus Avenue Baptist Church, and Eula hosted at least one Bible study at their new home. In 1940 they estimated the value of their new home at $7,500, quite moderate for a two-story house in Castle Heights. Possibly this reflects a fringe benefit of being an employee of Wm. Cameron & Co. ■

CHAPTER FOUR

Tudor Revival

186. Walter and Ida King House

2305 Morrow Avenue / 1923

In May 1924 Birch D. Easterwood marked eight years of work as an architect in Waco with an advertisement in the *Waco News-Tribune*. He listed a number of "Easterwood Landmarks," including the Liberty National Bank at Austin Avenue and Sixth Street (see *Historic Buildings*, 58), Brooks Hall at Baylor University (demolished), and several houses, including this one. A little more than a year earlier, Easterwood had announced that he was forming a partnership with Earl M. King, an Illinois native who had worked for a decade as a draftsman with Scott and Pearson, then Milton W. Scott & Company. Though the partnership with Easterwood was short-lived, it came at the time when the firm was designing this house.

Walter Blackburn King's father was an early Waco physician and surgeon, but he died in 1889, the very year that his son was born. His mother, Minnie Carroll King, moved back in with her father, Francis L. Carroll, who was the owner of a sawmill and the treasurer of Baylor University. In fact, the family moved to 705 Speight in 1898, then on the edge of the Baylor campus, perhaps in anticipation that young Walter would attend the university. That he did, playing on the baseball team and earning his bachelor of science degree in 1908. After a brief sojourn as a bookkeeper at Nash-Robinson & Company, he took a job with the Hanna-James-Taylor Company at 220 S. Second (see *Historic Buildings*, 47). He started as a shipping clerk and rose to manager of the shipping department. Around 1921 the company became the Meadows Company, and Walter continued his rise to assistant secretary and, by 1930, president.

Even after marrying Ida Stamps, a native of Seguin, the newlyweds lived with his mother on Speight. There they remained until at least 1917. While planning their new home, they rented a house one block away at 2216 Morrow. In the same block, the president of the Meadows Company, Claude W. Meadows, and his wife, Sue, were living at 2207 Morrow. (Both houses are still in existence.)

The house that Easterwood & King designed for Walter and Ida was highly sculptural. The main block was two stories and had two intersecting hipped roofs. Beyond this core was a two-story wing to the left (originally the first floor was open) and a one-story wing to the right. The house was quite eclectic: the hipped roofs and the veneer of red bricks could be found on any number of Colonial Revival houses in Waco, but the low Tudor arch of the one-story porch and the second-story oriel window to the right of this hinted at the Tudor Revival. This was early for

186. Walter and Ida
King House

the Tudor Revival in Waco—only the Clifton house by Milton W. Scott had been completed by 1923, and Easterwood would work on more fully developed versions of the style in the second Barclay house on Colcord and the Greene house on Maple (see *Historic Homes*, 88 and 99).

When they moved into this house, Walter was 33, and Ida 34. They had three children, Betty, Walter, and Frank; another child, Martha, would soon join them. Also in the household was Walter's mother, Minnie, who was 57. In 1920 the family had two live-in servants: house servant Ella Jahnke, who was white, and chauffeur Alvin V. Lemmons, who was black. In 1930 they had no live-in servants, even though they had built a hipped-roof garage with an apartment on the second story. They estimated the value of the house at $30,000. In 1940 that estimation of value had dropped to $10,000, thanks to the Great Depression. In that year the garage apartment was occupied by Carrie B. Smith, a widowed African American who worked as the King family's housekeeper. ◼

187. Howard and Olga Herrick House

3410 Chateau Avenue / 1925–26

This was the house of Howard Herrick and his wife, Olga. The Herrick family developed Castle Heights—first as a separate town, then as a subdivision in Waco—along with W. L. Wollet. Indeed, the name of the last street to be plotted in Castle Heights, Herwol, was a mash-up of Herrick and Wollet. W. T. Herrick owned a hardware store on the north side of the town square. The store sold hardware, both retail and wholesale, but also automobile accessories, agricultural implements, and tires. W. T. Herrick was also the secretary-treasurer of the Castle Heights Company; his eldest son, James S. Herrick, was vice president and also the manager of the Herrick Motor Company, which was at 1625 Bosque. The president of the Castle Heights Company was W. L. Wollet. Their offices in 1926 were south of the Square in the Hanna-James-Taylor Building at 212–220 S. Second (see *Historic Buildings*, 47).

187. Howard and Olga Herrick House

Howard Herrick, the younger son, was a clerk at Herrick Hardware. In 1921 Howard was single and living in his parents' house at 1700 West. After marrying Olga McLane, the newlyweds lived for a while in the Crawford Apartments at 2000 Austin Avenue (see 154 in this book). They were in this house by 1926. When the census taker visited in 1930, Howard was 29 and Olga was 28, and they had been married eight years. They had two young daughters, Marjorie Sue and Mary Elizabeth, who were 4 and 1. Also in the household was an African American servant, Rosa Taylor, who was 33 and divorced. Howard's profession was manager of an insurance company; Olga was unusual for her time in also having an occupation: assistant manager of an insurance company.

The house was stucco over a frame, either one story or one and a half stories, depending on which Sanborn Map one consults. The front porch was on the left side, which was also the side where the driveway ran; this front porch doubled as a porte cochere, though the driveway was not covered. The entrance was a round-arched door on the side wall, which led directly into the living room. The presence of a chimney centered within the front gable indicated that a fireplace was on the other side of this wall. The one-story garage was at the left rear corner.

When the Sanborn Map was drawn in 1926, this house and the Orand house at 3415 (see the next entry) were the only two houses on this block. By the time the map was updated in 1950, the block was pretty much filled. ■

188. J. Bruton and Frances Orand House

3415 Chateau Avenue   /   1925–26

James Bruton Orand was the son of James W. Orand, vice president of the Herrick Hardware Company. Bruton was working as a clerk at the hardware store by 1913 while living with his parents at 1512 Columbus. After his father died, Bruton lived with the W. T. Herrick family at 1700 West, even after he began to work for the Nash-Waco Company around 1923. (In 1920 he was listed as living with his widowed mother at 2715 Sanger.) The Nash-Waco Company was the local distributor for Nash and Cadillac automobiles, with a showroom at 822 Austin Avenue (now a

188. J. Bruton and Frances Orand House

parking lot). Around this time Bruton married Frances Nash, whose father, Joseph Nash, had founded the company.

Being so close to the Herrick family, both professionally and personally, it was perhaps inevitable that Bruton and Frances would be early residents of Castle Heights, which was developed by W. T. Herrick and W. L. Wollet. Bruton turned to Birch D. Easterwood, the rising star among Waco architects. Easterwood was working on the design in the summer of 1925, and by September he had completed drawings for a one-story, six-room house, framed and covered with stucco, which was to cost $7,000.

Apparently Bruton, or perhaps Frances, or perhaps her parents, thought that they were aiming too low, and soon Easterwood was expanding the scheme. By December he had come up with a two-story version, which would cost $9,000. In February 1926 the contact was awarded to Townley & Trimmier of Waco, who agreed to build it for $8,000. The company consisted of Robert M. Townley and T. Leslie Trimmier, carpenters; this house is their only known commission.

The house was fairly low key. The main roof ran parallel to the street. The house seems to be one story, but there were multiple windows in a shed dormer and in an equilateral gable. A lower gable was under the upper gable, with the right slope of both roofs aligning. The door was recessed behind a round arch; the door itself came to a low triangular point, something of a halfhearted attempt at Tudor styling. The door also had applied metal straps that aspired to look like strap hinges, another medieval-ish touch. The chimney on the right side of the main block marked the living room.

The wing on the right side was not in the original phase of construction but was present by 1950. At the back property line there was a one-story garage but no apartment; one was added before 1950.

The Orand family lived in the house for about a decade. By 1940 they were living in the Stoneleigh Apartments in Dallas; Bruton was president of a Buick dealership there. ■

189. Wilton and Ethel Lanning House (Lanning-Stevens House)

3721 Austin Avenue / Circa 1929

When it was built, this house was the last on Austin Avenue and remained the farthest out for quite a while. The original owners were Wilton A. Lanning Sr. and Ethel Carrie Spencer Lanning. Wilton, who became a Waco banker, was a native of Mexia, some forty-two miles east of East. Ethel was the daughter of Richard Boyd Spencer and Mary Catherine Lattimore and was born in Dublin, Texas, ninety miles northwest of Waco. Ethel grew up in the family's Victorian house at the corner of Columbus Avenue and Fourteenth Street, and they were strong supporters of the neighboring Baptist church.

When Wilton and Ethel were married, they lived for several years with Wilton's widowed mother at 1725 Morrow. Around 1929 they built this house and were all moved in when the census taker came on April 14, 1930. They estimated the value of the house at $25,000, which must have been pretty accurate given how recently the house had been built. However, for several

189. Wilton and Ethel
Lanning House (Lanning-
Stevens House)

years they lived at 1324 Columbus, taking care of Ethel's mom, Catherine. (Catherine died in February 1938, and the family gave the house to the church; it was later demolished to allow for the expansion of the church complex.) During those years Wilton and Ethel rented 3721 Austin to Irving M. Griffin, who worked for cotton brokers George H. McFadden and Brothers. All this time Wilton was working for the First National Bank, progressing from bookkeeper to clerk to teller to assistant cashier. Wilton and Ethel had two children: Elizabeth, born in 1927, and Wilton Jr., born in 1936.

The house was built by N. A. Palmer, a contractor; the blueprints give only his name, not the name of an architect. Norman A. Palmer was born and grew up in Nebraska; he worked as

a carpenter in Lincoln. He moved his family to Graham, Texas, in the 1910s and moved to Waco around 1925; in that year he was 48 years old. Between 1920 and 1930 he shifted the title of his occupation from "carpenter" to "contractor." By 1930 his eldest son, James, 26, was working with him in the business.

In Waco he found work quickly; in 1925 he won the contracts for the Sallie Proctor McLendon house at 2912 Austin and the Abram and Birdie Patton house at 2402 Colcord, both designed by Birch D. Easterwood (see *Historic Homes*, 66 and 64). He also built houses in Castle Heights, including the Addison Baker and Frances Duncan house at 3804 Castle (see *Historic Homes*, 109). In the mid-1930s Palmer built a cottage for Graves and Alice Darby at 3502 Carondolet (see 203 in this book) and a much more imposing house for Hilton and Louise Howell at 3718 Herwol, designed by Birch D. Easterwood (see *Historic Homes*, 117).

This house showed a concern for stylishness, though not necessarily all of the same style. The tall, hipped roof, covered in fireproof slate, could have covered any Colonial Revival house, but beneath it were a variety of Tudor Revival features. The two-story gabled left bay of the house projected forward subtly, and the one-story covered porch projects forward a bit more. At the right side was a one-story porch, which was later enclosed. The wood frame was covered with a brick veneer, allowing windows to be clustered in threes across the façade. Such a treatment was very modern, and the six-over-six sash windows were characteristic of the late-colonial and early-national periods in America.

Inside, entry was directly into the living room, which stretched to the right. A fireplace was the focal point on the end wall, with a neoclassical mantel. An opening on the back wall led to the staircase—again, neoclassical—which also provided access to the side porch. To the left of the living room was the dining room, lit by windows in front and on the west side. A swinging door, typical of well-to-do Waco houses at this time, led to a pantry and the kitchen beyond. As usual on such houses, the master bedroom was above the living room, with triple windows facing the street and a side window and side door onto the deck created by the roof of the one-story porch. A master bathroom was above the entrance, lit by one small window. An east-west hallway connects with two additional bedrooms over the dining room and kitchen.

The house also had a separate garage covered in shingles, an allusion to New England vernacular buildings of the colonial era. This version was originally one story, with an apartment for a servant. Sometime after 1950 the building was given a second story, which created a new apartment upstairs and a two-car garage beneath. In 1930 the occupant was Theresa Thompson, a 23-year-old black woman who worked as a cook. (She was a widow, which might have made this job attractive.) The door to the garage apartment lined up with the door into the kitchen, so the walk across was the entirety of her commute. In 1940 the servant was Edna Davis, a 22-year-old white woman who was a native of New Jersey. She had attended high school for two years and was working as the family's maid.

After World War II, the Lannings sold the house to Frank F. and Elizabeth Bohart (Nell) Stevens and settled into a cottage at 2501 Colcord. Ethel Lanning's brother, Harry Spencer, lived across Twenty-Fifth Street in a two-story Foursquare (see 146 in this book). The Lanning house burned after they sold it in the 1960s. Their son Wilton Jr. attended Waco High and Baylor and became the president of Tom Padgitt, Inc. He was a highly public-spirited individual and was a cofounder of the Dr Pepper Museum and a supporter of many other cultural institutions. He also remained a member and supporter of Columbus Avenue Baptist Church.

When he bought this house, Frank F. Stevens was manager of the wholesale and manufacturing department of Wm. Cameron & Company; within a year he was executive vice president of the division and soon vice president of the entire company. (For other homes of Cameron employees, see *Historic Homes*, 48; and 153 and 171 in this volume.) By 1953 Frank and his son, Frank B., had founded the Frank Stevens Sash & Door Company. (Such products had been part of his purview with the Cameron Company.) By 1953 Frank Bohart Stevens and his wife, Margaret, were living at 3821 Chateau, which still stands though drastically remodeled; by 1968 they had moved to Acorn Drive. Frank F. died in 1959, but Elizabeth lived there for several years, though she later moved to a home for seniors. ◼

3434 Chateau Avenue   /   1930

Like the roof on the Orand house at 3415 Chateau, the steep main roof of this house ran parallel to the street. Unlike the front of the Orand house, two tall gables at the ends of the main block projected forward to frame the porch and the front door. The first-floor walls were all a brick veneer, while the upper part of all gables were covered with stucco, sometimes with wooden boards creating a pattern that echoed Tudor half-timbering. On the rear was a very wide shed dormer, which allowed for a great deal of usable space on the upper level. In the brick-veneered portion of the wall some bricks were raised, giving the surface added texture, especially with a raking light.

The large front windows were casements, not old-fashioned wooden casements but newfangled iron ones. Such windows were also used in the nearby Duncan house at 3804 Castle Avenue, built soon after the Tanenbaum house (see *Historic Homes*, 109). These modern windows in turn became old-fashioned and were replaced circa 2021. The chimney at the left end of the main block indicated that the living room was at that end of the house.

Originally, a porch ran across the back of the house; this porch has since been enclosed. The low wing to the left of the main block was originally the garage; behind it was a small apartment. In recent times a hipped-roof parking structure was built, and the former garage was converted into living space.

The house was built for Nat and Mildred Tanenbaum. Nat, a New York native with German roots, was originally a cotton broker, but by 1940 he was a stockbroker. For many years his office was in the Liberty National Bank Building at Austin Avenue and Sixth Street (see *Historic Buildings*, 58). Mildred was a native of Tennessee. In 1930, the year they moved into this house, Nat was 44 and Mildred was 37, and they had two children, Elizabeth (Betty), 9, and Nat Jr., 7. Nat was a high school graduate, while Mildred had two years of college. By 1940 Betty was a junior in college and Nat Jr. was a sophomore.

The family was Presbyterian, and Nat served many years as a deacon. He was also an ardent athlete and a major supporter of the YMCA. In 1930 the apartment to the rear was occupied by their maid, Bertha Drews, a single, 28-year-old woman born in Texas to German immigrants. She had moved on by 1932, and the Tanenbaums had difficulty finding a maid willing to take the apartment as part of her compensation. Finally, in 1938 they found Lillie M. Smith, but she was replaced the next year by Ida M. Washington, who also did not stay long.

The Tanenbaums were visited by the census taker soon after they moved in, so the $27,000 cost of the house was still fresh in their mind. This was much higher than either the Herrick house ($15,000) or the Orand house ($8,000). After ten years of the Great Depression, the Tanenbaum house was valued at $10,000. ◼

190. Nat and Mildred Tanenbaum House

191. Harlon and Clara Fentress House
(Fentress-Hoehn House)

3722 Chateau Avenue   /   1930

Built for Harlon and Clara (Lacy) Fentress, this house blended the Tudor Revival with aspects of the arts and crafts movement as practiced in California. Harlon Fentress was born in Norwalk, Ohio, and came to Texas with his parents, Ephraim and Edith Fentress, in 1914; Ephraim was publisher of the *Waco News-Tribune* and the *Waco Times-Herald*. Harlon attended the University of Texas, where he met Clara Lacy, a native of Dallas who was also studying business. They married in 1924 and were longtime members of Columbus Avenue Baptist Church. Harlon worked in the family business: in 1932 he was the manager of national advertising for the Waco newspapers.

Gus Olson took the contract to build this house in January 1930. Only five years before this Gus had built the house of Harlon's parents, Ephraim and Edith (see *Historic Homes*, 65). The name of the architect is not mentioned in the lien; it might be Herman F. Cason, who had designed the house of the elder Fentresses. (The name T. Brooks Pearson has been suggested, which is a possibility, but Cason had been a draftsman for Pearson before, during, and after Pearson's partnership with Milton W. Scott.)

The combination of stone and clinker brick (brick intentionally burned and/or given an irregular form) recalled the California version of the arts and crafts movement, both in Southern California with Greene and Greene and in the Bay Area with Bernard Maybeck. Tudor arches were often used throughout the interior. The living room, a double-height space to the left of the entry hall, featured exposed beams with turned king posts. The fireplace was on the side wall, with appropriate Tudor detailing.

This was one of the earliest houses in Waco to have a garage attached to the main house rather than as a separate outbuilding; as a result, the servant's quarter was above the garage but attached to the main house. (Another small dwelling in the backyard was noted on the 1950 Sanborn Map, but that no longer exists.) Less than ten years later, Harlan and Clara built another house one block away at 3820 Chateau.

By 1939 their old house was the home of pediatrician F. William Hoehn; his wife, Gertrude Curtis Hoehn; and their two daughters. Dr. Hoehn's offices were on the eighteenth floor of the ALICO building (see *Historic Buildings*, 55). Dr. Hoehn's mother, Charlotte Hoehn, was a wealthy widow who had built 2715 Austin Avenue in 1923–24 (see *Historic Homes*, 68). William and Curtis lived with her for a while but by 1930 were living at 1809 Sanger Avenue. In 1940 they estimated the value of the house at $15,000, which was probably accurate given that they had purchased it only a year or two before. A house like this would have been worth $25,000 ten years earlier, before the Great Depression. ■

191. Harlon and Clara Fentress House (Fentress-Hoehn House)

192. George and Lillie Liddell House

2800 Maple Avenue   /   1933–34

George Liddell was a native of Alabama who became a physician and moved to Texas. After moving to Waco he worked at the Colgin Hospital on Columbus, then in private practice, and then as city physician and health officer. His wife, Lillie, was a clerk at the US Post Office, a position she kept for many years. In their early years in Waco they rented a house at 1912 Washington for fifty dollars a month.

In September 1924 Dr. Liddell talked with Birch Easterwood about making plans for a two-story, seven-room frame house, but such talks, it seems, were premature. Not until November 1933 did they return to Easterwood and resume planning their dream house. Sadly, they had little time to enjoy the house together, as Dr. Liddell died in 1938 at the age of 54. Lillie sold the house to her brother-in-law, Dan H. Tudort, and her sister, Anne. Dan was the manager of a farm implement company.

The house seems to be one story, but the gable on the right above the entrance reaches close to a full second story. The brick wall corbels out to both sides, making for a wider and more emphatic roofline. The window to the right of the door, placed halfway between the first and second floors, lit the landing of the staircase. The chimney stack to the left of the door indicated the location of the living room. The pair of dormers that rise from the roof are matched by a pair on the rear side of the roof, indicating a room similar to the upstairs room above the living room in Easterwood's own house (see *Historic Homes*, 97). The frame house of 1924 was now a brick-veneered house of 1934. Its irregularity was considered a virtue, part and parcel of the Tudor style. ◼

192. George and Lillie Liddell House

Mediterranean and Spanish Colonial Revival

193. Valley View, the Summer Residence of William Waldo and Helen Cameron (later Art Center Waco)

1300 College Drive   /   Circa 1922–24

This was the country home—and more specifically, the summer residence—of William Waldo Cameron and his second wife, Helen Miller Cameron. But it was not the first Cameron summer residence at this location. The property was named Valley View Farm by its previous owner, Dr. Willis N. Rogers, a recent arrival to Waco who was a physician and surgeon in the late 1890s. Dr. Rogers was in declining health and died April 30, 1900. His widow, Jennie, was involved in a lawsuit about the ownership of the farm, which was settled in her favor in June 1903. Soon thereafter, William Waldo Cameron purchased Valley View Farm, which was his favorite place on earth for the rest of his life.

His parents, William and Flora Cameron, came to Waco in the late 1870s. William Cameron was soon building an empire of lumber; in the earliest years he had W. W. Larmour design a Second Empire house on Austin Avenue (see *Historic Homes*, p. 5.) It was stylish and substantial but not overbearing. This was where William Waldo Cameron and his two sisters, Flora and Margaret, grew up. William Cameron Sr. died in 1899, and William Waldo, though in his early twenties, rapidly took over the company. His sister Flora married Frank Burkett Baird, an industrialist from Buffalo, in November 1900. In January 1901 William Waldo married Frank's sister, Faith; Walter G. Lacy of Waco was his best man. (Margaret stayed closer to home, marrying Edward R. Bolton.)

William Waldo and Faith lived for years with his mom in the house built by his dad. The acquisition of Valley View Farm allowed them a space of their own. They soon built a country house, simply known as Valley View, on a bluff overlooking the Bosque River and farmland beyond—a view now diminished by the sideroad detritus of Interstate 35. This house was two stories with a gambrel roof (i.e., a roof with two pitches, the upper slope more shallow than the lower), allowing for a very spacious attic. The walls (as well as the roof) were clad in wooden shingles in what has become known as the Shingle style. This had become one of the go-to styles for up-scale oceanfront houses in New England and for country houses in Upstate New

York. The use of shingles on steep roofs and on walls gave such houses an informal and very natural appearance. When the census taker came by Valley View on May 2, 1910, William Waldo and Faith were living there with their daughter, Eleanor, and three servants. William's sister Margaret; her husband, Edward; and their child were living with her mother on Austin Avenue.

In that year William and Faith were talking with architect Roy E. Lane about designing a town house for them. This was built in 1911–12 at 1717 Austin (see *Historic Homes*, p. 10). This house would not have been out of place in Newport, Rhode Island, or some other haunt of the very well-to-do. The first reception was in February 1912, but William and Faith continued to entertain at Valley View for dance parties and other occasions. The way in which both 1717 Austin and the Shingle-style summer home reflected East Coast tastes may suggest that New Yorker Faith was making her preferences known; or it may be that William Waldo was attempting to make his New Yorker wife more comfortable living in faraway Texas.

Sometime in late 1920 or early 1921 William Waldo and Faith Cameron were divorced. Their daughter, Eleanor, had been attending Miss Bennett's School in Millbrook, New York, about ninety miles north of New York City. Faith moved to New York City and lived in an apartment on Park Avenue for many years. In the fall of 1921 she took a trip to Europe, and on the ship's register she listed herself as a widow. In 1923 she married Samuel Cole, who was in real estate and made much of his money buying and flipping houses in Lenox, Massachusetts. One of these he gave to Faith, who spent a great deal of money fixing it up, only to have her husband sell it. Faith asked for and received a divorce in Reno, Nevada; she never remarried but remained Faith Cole for the rest of her life.

Meanwhile, back in Waco, Eleanor was named Cotton Palace Queen in the fall of 1921. (The Cotton Palace was Waco's unique blend of a county fair and a debutante ball.) This required a whirl of social occasions at the Cameron house on Austin Avenue, at the summer residence, and at the Hotel Raleigh. Faith Cameron was conspicuous by her absence.

On June 21, 1922, William Waldo married a local girl, Helen Miller, in St. Paul's Episcopal Church. She was not just any local girl, however. Her mother Flora's father was W. D. Lacy, a prominent cotton merchant, coal dealer, and banker. Her brother Walter married Lucile Roane Cooper, whose father had founded the Cooper wholesale grocery business, so they were well connected with the upper levels of Waco society. Helen was much younger than William Waldo—he was 44 when they married, and she was 24. In fact, she was three years older than his daughter, Eleanor.

Family recollections say that the new summer house was built for the wedding of William Waldo and Helen. However, a *Waco News-Tribune* article of April 2, 1922, included photos of both the Austin Avenue house and the original summer house, with no indication that it was about to be replaced. An early history of Wm. Cameron & Company, which is undated but included a photo of Helen in her bridal dress, showed photos of both the old and new summer residences, as well as one devoted solely to the view of the valley. The new house must have been completed not long after the wedding—sometime between late 1922 and 1924. It seems that William Waldo concluded that he wanted a fresh start, with a new wife and a new summer residence.

193. Valley View, the Summer Residence of William Waldo and Helen Cameron (later Art Center Waco)

The new house apparently was on the same site as the older one, where the land dropped off sharply to the north and east. The rear of the house took advantage of the view to the northeast, while the other faced a new feature: an in-ground swimming pool. On that southwestern side three French doors opened onto a covered loggia, the roof of which was supported by four white classical columns. This loggia was also framed by projecting end bays. The walls were covered with stucco, and the roof covered with red tiles, giving it the appearance of a Mediterranean villa. William Waldo may well have been aware of Laguna Gloria, the suburban villa of Clara Driscoll Sevier in Austin, built in 1916 to the designs of Harvey L. Page. This was a much larger and more sophisticated treatment, especially the side that faced the Colorado River, now Lake Austin.

The original part of the house is the central section: wings were added later, and, indeed, the photos in the Cameron Company history suggest that it originally had just one main story. However, the pool is well documented in those pictures. An in-ground swimming pool, extraordinarily rare in 1920s Waco, was bounded by a pergola, with white classical columns that matched those on the loggia. The pergola was aligned with the end bays that projected forward from the main block so that pairs of squarish paver stones could run from each side door between the columns all the way around the pool. The diving board was at the end of the pool closest to the house. At some time the opposite end was formalized with two cabanas where guests could change into their swimsuits.

William Waldo and Helen used the summer residence to hold family events and entertain in an intimate fashion: a bridge party, a tea party, or, of course, a pool party. The house was sometimes used for events related to the family business. This might be a picnic for company employees and their families—one such event in April 1928 hosted seven hundred people plus an orchestra and vaudeville performers. It could also be used for promoting economic growth in Waco. In June 1928 the Chamber of Commerce held its annual banquet on the rooftop of the Raleigh Hotel. The next afternoon fifty visiting businessmen and guest-of-honor Jesse Jones of Houston were hosted at Valley View Farm. One photo showed Helen seated next to Jones, the Houston businessman who would serve on the board of the Reconstruction Finance Corporation under Herbert Hoover and Franklin D. Roosevelt and later as FDR's secretary of commerce.

The glory days of Valley View Farm ended with the death of William Waldo Cameron from a heart attack in October 1939. His funeral service was held at Valley View, and a newspaper article commented that "Mr. Cameron's greatest pleasures in life were his business, his family, his country home and outdoor recreation, which included hunting, fishing and horses." In November 1940 Helen married the Reverend Everett H. Jones, who had been rector of St. Paul's in Waco from 1930 to 1938 and was now rector of St. Mark's Episcopal in San Antonio, the church in which he had grown up. Helen returned to Valley View from time to time, but these visits became more difficult when her husband was named bishop of El Paso in 1943.

Eleanor Cameron, the daughter of William Waldo and Faith, remained on the East Coast. In 1929 she married Courtlandt Van Clief, who was president of a gravel, sand, and limestone company—an occupation not far off from her father's. At first they lived in New York and had a daughter, Faith, named for Eleanor's mother. In 1940 they were living in Palm Beach, Florida; by 1950 they lived on a country estate, Verulam, near Charlottesville, Virginia.

In 1966 the house and 160 acres of farmland surrounding it were sold for the creation of McLennan Community College (MCC). The old Cameron summer house was rented out on a long-term basis as the home of Art Center Waco. The prominent San Antonio architectural firm Ford, Powell & Carson was tasked with turning the house into ten thousand square feet of space for exhibits, classes, and administration. Milton Babbitt, the architect in charge, noted that it had a prime site with a beautiful setting and easy access to plenty of parking.

The exterior of the house provided most of its charm, which meant that the interior could be freely remodeled. Though the basic structure remained the same, virtually no original windows or doors remained. Perhaps an even bigger change was filling in the pool to create a courtyard. Ford, Powell & Carson planned for new galleries between the pergola and the parking lot and between the two cabanas at the far end of the pool. These galleries were never built, and the house was used intensively over the years.

In October 2017 the building was closed when structural problems were discovered. These problems, while serious, may well derive from years if not decades of deferred maintenance, which often sound the death knell for historic buildings owned by institutions. The lease to Art Center Waco was nearing an end, and the institution decided to purchase a property at 701 S. Eighth Street in downtown Waco. This was a site more likely to draw visitors, especially given its proximity to the Magnolia Market. MCC administrators have struggled to find a new purpose for the building, and its fate is uncertain at this writing. ■

194. Veterans Administration Hospital Staff Quarters

4800 Memorial Drive   /   1931–32

The Veterans Administration Hospital, built in 1931–32, had residential quarters at the northern corner of the property near the point where New Road and Beverly Drive would one day intersect. Like the rest of the hospital complex (see *Historic Buildings*, 69), the four residential structures are all in a uniform style, which would have been called Italian Renaissance when they were built but which now are classed in the broader stylistic category of Mediterranean Revival. All have redbrick walls and red tile roofs, with minimal applied decoration. However, the buildings were well designed, blending functional needs with attention to the forms and proportion of the individual units. All four buildings had exposed rafter ends, a feature that was a holdover from the arts and crafts movement.

Building 19 was the "MOC residence," that is, a single-family residence for the medical officer in charge. It faced due north toward the corner of the property. The main block was two stories tall, resting atop a raised basement and three bays wide; although it was balanced and dignified, it was also subtly asymmetrical. This building was the longtime residence of Dr. Harry Rubin,

194. Veterans Administration Hospital Staff Quarters

the first medical officer in charge, and his wife, Mary Gough Rubin. A native of Waycross, Georgia, Rubin earned his medical degree from the University of Pennsylvania, where he may have met his future wife, who was a native of Harrisburg, Pennsylvania. He served as a major in the Medical Corps during World War I and, after a brief time in private practice, joined the Veterans Administration. He was stationed at several hospitals in the Southeast and the West before being named MOC at Waco.

Dr. Rubin took charge on January 16, 1932, and thus oversaw the completion of phase 1 of the hospital. In his seventeen years of service, he oversaw the two major expansions of the hospital, comprising most of the buildings now in the National Register Historic District. Harry was Jewish, and Mary Presbyterian, but they seem to have worked out a respect for each other's faith traditions. Mary died in 1941 and was buried with her family back in Harrisburg. Dr. Rubin rejoined the Medical Corps during World War II, rising to the rank of colonel. After the war he resumed work in Waco until he was forced by physical ailments to retire in 1949. When he died in 1957, the funeral service was jointly officiated by Charles T. Caldwell of First Presbyterian and Rabbi Amiel Wohl of Rodef Sholom; he was buried in San Antonio at Fort Sam Houston National Cemetery.

Facing northeast was Building 18, which was built as quarters for nurses. It consisted of two stories atop a basement. The aboveground part of the basement had a facing of stone, while the main floors were brick. Because it was a long building, the architects used gabled pavilions at both ends to give variety as well as formality. The central entrance was marked by a one-story porch covered with a tile roof, and at both narrow ends were arcaded porches. These shady porches must have been popular gathering spots for off-duty nurses in non-air-conditioned Waco. The end pavilions and the arcaded porches also featured decorative brickwork above the window openings and arches. Even the picturesque chimney had arched openings on all sides and a tiny tile roof.

Facing to the northwest were Buildings 20 and 21; these were intended to be "officer duplexes" for other senior staff members. Both buildings were six bays wide; each building consisted of two residences, each three bays with a central door as the focal point. On each duplex one door was set within a round arch, while the other was set in a projecting one-story bay with a red tile roof. The formal front contrasted with the projecting porches on the rear façade. Again, there was a raised basement, faced with brick, linking it to Building 19 rather than Building 18. On each side elevation were one-story porches or sunrooms. On each end of the roof were pairs of chimneys with brick hoods, connected by a blind arch. Without spending much money on applied ornament, the architects designed a group of residential buildings that were beautiful as well as functional. ■

195. Harry and Sadie Kestner House

3601 Austin Avenue / 1935

The Kestner family arrived in Waco around 1912 and appeared for the first time in the Waco city directories in 1913. Samuel Kestner opened a dry goods store on the south side of the town square. Samuel and his wife, Rachel, moved into 1821 Columbus Avenue, a simple two-story house with a double gallery in front—now an empty lot. His two sons, Isaac and Harry, were both clerks in the store in 1913. Brother Isaac (Ike) bought the old Cornish Building on Elm Avenue in East Waco and opened his own dry goods store (see *Historic Buildings*, 20). Eventually he and his wife, Katie, hired Birch Easterwood to design a house for them at 3724 Chateau (see *Historic Homes*, 110).

Harry became the son in S. Kestner & Son. In 1920 Harry was a newlywed; he and his bride, Sadie, were living with Richard and Ina Jurney at 325 N. Tenth Street, but they soon moved into 2008 N. Seventh, where they lived for about fifteen years. In the 1920s Harry became the proprietor of his own dry goods store, first on Franklin and then for many years on the north side of the Square. Early in 1935, when Harry was in his early forties and Sadie in her mid-thirties, they hired longtime Waco architect T. Brooks Pearson to design this house.

195. Harry and Sadie Kestner House

Pearson, a native of Georgia, had been the second partner of Milton W. Scott. In their brief partnership they designed the Shear-Callan and Smith-Parker-Migel houses on Columbus Avenue (see *Historic Homes*, 33) and oversaw the construction of Waco High School. Around 1920 he withdrew from practice and became a gentleman farmer, but he was back to architecture by 1928. Perhaps his most prominent design was the Central Fire Station and Drill Tower on Columbus (see *Historic Buildings*, 68), an essay in the Spanish Colonial, and he also oversaw the construction of the Coca-Cola Bottling Co. building on Austin (see *Historic Buildings*, 53).

By 1935 he was busy enough to employ two draftsmen: Walter Cocke Jr., 31, and G. Robert Olson, 28. Cocke's father was a prominent Waco attorney and judge (see *Historic Homes*, 22), and Bob Olson was the son of Waco contractor Gustav Olson. For the Kestner project, Cocke and Olson divided the work: Cocke produced the plot plan, the foundation and basement plan, and the first-floor plan; while Olson drafted up the front and east-side elevation on one sheet, the rear and west-side elevation on another, and a sheet filled with details on the third. All six sheets were dated March 4, 1935. One week later, Cocke and Olson announced that they were forming a partnership, with their office at 1503 Franklin Avenue.

Like the house of his brother Ike, this house can be characterized as Mediterranean Revival, as many of its features might be found in Italy but also in Spain. The house was one story but sat well above street level; moreover, the ground sloped down to the rear. This allowed for a half-basement with a three-car garage, a game room, and a large laundry room. Basement-level garages had also been used on the Bruce and Yvonne Duncan house and more recently at the Garrett house, both on Austin Avenue (see *Historic Homes*, 76 and 114). The walls were built of tile blocks, veneered with a light tan brick. The roof was covered with red tiles, one of the basic features of Mediterranean houses. Two chimneys rose from the roof, one serving the right front room and another heating the entry hall and the room behind it.

The front porch, created by three round arches, was framed by wings that projected forward. (This arrangement was similar to the Quebe house at 3024 Novice Road; see *Historic Homes*, 105.) The path to the front door was not centered but ran on the right side of the lawn near the driveway. The three arches of the porch were supported by an outer pair of Doric piers and an inner pair of cast-stone columns with spiraling shafts, known as the Solomonic order, for the columns supposed to have been used in King Solomon's Temple in Jerusalem. The right wing had a large window under a round arch; the matching window on the left wing had a grouping of casements, covered now (and probably originally) by a canvas awning.

There were three doors on the covered part of the front porch. That on the right opened into the living room, that in the center into the library, and that on the left into the master bedroom. The living room had a large arched window on the south and one window on each side of the fireplace on the east wall. The north end of the living room received special attention. The wall had three arches, the middle one taller and wider, supported by two more cast-stone Solomonic columns. In the outer arches were wrought-iron railings and in the middle arch, wrought-iron gates. Two oak steps led to the dining room, and another two led to the library. That room had a fireplace opposite the door to the porch (like the fireplace in the living room, gas) and two bookshelves on the west wall. Behind the library were the kitchen and a breakfast room. On the west side the master bedroom was in front, with a separate dressing room and bathroom; at the north end was a second bedroom with its own bath.

On September 20, 1936, the new house was used for a fund-raising event—"a benefit tea"—for Senior Hadassah. (This organization of American Jewish women, founded in 1912, took as their own the birth name of Queen Esther.) The funds were to go to Youth Aliyah, a project to remove young people ages 16 and 17 from Germany to Palestine, "where they will be given a two-year vocational course, enabling them to make a living." In their own small way, the Jewish women of Waco took a stand against the persecution of Jewish people in Germany, the persecution that culminated in the Holocaust, and this house played a role in the attempt to lead some youth to the promised land. ▪

196. Herman and Carrie Cason House

2900 Columbus Avenue   /   1941

Herman F. Cason was born in Meridian, the county seat of Bosque County, northwest of Waco. His family moved to Waco in the 1890s, and his father, Joseph F. Cason, pursued a career as a carpenter and contractor. Herman thus had building in his blood, and by the age of 17 he was working as a draftsman for T. B. Pearson. He stayed with Pearson when his boss formed a partnership with Milton W. Scott and remained with Pearson after the partnership broke up. When Pearson decided on what turned out to be a premature retirement, Cason and fellow draftsman E. McIver Ross took over the projects on hand as Ross & Cason. With Ross, Cason designed the Texas Telephone Company Exchange on North Ninth. By 1919, Ross and Cason went their separate ways. Cason designed St. John's Methodist Church at Eighteenth and Bosque but specialized in houses.

All this time Herman was living with his parents in their Queen Anne cottage on North Eighteenth Street, very near St. John's. (The family were devoted Methodists.) Herman did not marry until he was 36 years old. His bride was Carrie Allen, who grew up in Valley Mills but moved to Waco with her family in 1921. For many years Carrie was a teacher at the Sanger Avenue School, which was unusual but must have seemed a godsend when the Great Depression slowed construction and thus work for Herman. Carrie and Herman lived for a few years at 519 N. Twenty-Fifth Street, which they rented for thirty-five dollars a month, then at 2301 N. Fifteenth Street, before moving around the corner to 1210 Herring Avenue. This was a good location for a Methodist couple, as it was just east of the Herring Avenue Methodist Church and across the street from the Methodist Children's Home. Herman moved his office from downtown to this house to save more money.

In addition to Carrie's steady income from teaching, Herman found some work supervising the Civilian Conservation Corps in erecting Mother Neff State Park near McGregor and working for a year or two as Waco's building inspector. In 1939 he won a few new commissions to design houses and also to design the new Elite Café at the Circle for the Colias brothers (see *Historic Buildings*, 39). Apparently Herman and Carrie felt that they could build a new house for themselves. Their lot at 2900 Columbus was at the edge of Waco, but the Karem Park Addition and Castle Heights were just to the west. (The house predates St. Alban's Episcopal Church, at the other end of the block, which was built after World War II; see *Historic Buildings*, 16.)

Presumably Herman designed their new home, though it was different from the Colonial Revival, Southern Colonial, and English cottages that he had designed for others. The two-story house might best be called Mediterranean Revival, somewhere between the Spanish Colonial and the Italian. The house had a wooden frame (which helped with costs) covered with stucco; the main roof was red tile. (The little front porch was apparently a later addition.) The front elevation was asymmetrical, though the main block and the slightly lower entrance block each had a symmetrical arrangement of windows. All of the windows were casements. Amazingly, all of the original windows seem to have survived, perhaps because they were custom-made and of an unusual shape. The house was U-shaped in plan, with the wings framing an open arcade. At the end of the western wing was a small garage.

The Casons were still listed as living on South Twelfth in the 1941 city directory, but they moved into the new house sometime that year. Tragically, Herman had a heart attack in the new house on November 21 and died at age 51. Carrie continued to live in the house for a few years and continued to teach at the Sanger Avenue School, but by 1945 she had moved back to the house on Herring Avenue, where she was joined by her brother, Thomas, and sister, Kate Batson. She died in 1988, joining Herman in Oakwood Cemetery.

196. Herman and Carrie Cason House

CHAPTER SIX

Period Cottages

197. Albert and Esther Gugenheim House (Gugenheim-Trautschold House)

2901 Sanger Avenue / 1924

This handsome Tudor Revival cottage anchored the corner of Sanger and Twenty-Ninth. The steeply pitched main roof ran from side to side—that is, east to west—and a wing projected forward on the west, with a trio of windows and the obligatory bit of half-timbering in the gable. The east slope of this roof intersected with the western portion of the gable over the front door. On the side wall of the western wing a narrow French door opened onto the uncovered porch. The front door itself was set back from the round-arched opening, and a chimney with two stacks rose to the right of that opening. The frontal placement of a chimney usually indicates that the living room is on the other side of this wall. On the eastern end of house was another tripartite window set within a Tudor arch.

The brickwork was enlivened by the inclusion of a fair number of dark bricks and by the placement of many bricks on their short ends—that is, headers—to contrast with the bricks laid longways, known as stretchers. Headers were used to bond outer and inner walls in load-bearing brick walls, whereas the use of all stretchers was a sign that they were a veneer resting on a frame of wood. In fact, this is one of the few houses in Waco to have alternating rows of headers and stretchers. The Sanborn mapmaker noticed this and marked the house as having solid brick walls rather than a veneer.

This was one of those rare Waco houses that was designed by an out-of-town architect. Wilford S. Bogue of Fort Worth had completed the plans for the house by April 1924. Bogue was born in Kentucky, but both his parents were natives of Indiana, across the Ohio River to the north. His widowed mother, Mary F. Bogue, had moved to Fort Worth by 1910, when Wilford was 9. He graduated from high school and by age 19 was calling himself an architect, though he does not appear as such in a city directory until 1924. (This was an age when many architects did not attend architecture school but were educated by working in a senior architect's office.) Though Bogue never rose to the first ranks of Fort Worth architects, the Gugenheim-Trautschold house showed him to be a capable designer of houses.

Bogue's clients were Albert D. and Esther Gugenheim. Both were born in Texas; Albert's father was a native of Alabama, and his mother of Texas; Esther's father was born in Mississippi,

and her mother in the District of Columbia. They were new arrivals to Waco; in 1923 they were living in the Palm Court Apartments, which had just opened in 1921. Albert worked for the San Antonio Machine and Supply Company, which made engines, boilers, cotton gin machinery, and oil mill supplies. In 1930 there were five family members living here: Albert, 42; Esther, 36; their son, Albert D. Jr., who went by Dick, 11; daughter, Bette Ann, 7; and mother-in-law, Hattie Carb, 64. There was also a garage with an apartment, where Julia Kolb, 17, who worked as their maid, lived. She was a native Texan, as was her mother, but her father was a native of Austria.

In 1928 the house next door at 2905 Sanger was under construction for Emmette J. Oates Jr., the secretary-treasurer of a steel plant, and his wife, Gladys. Next door to them at 2917 were Harry Gorman, a retail grocer, and his wife, Fay. And across Sanger at 2900 was Turner E. Hubby and his wife, Mattie; Turner was a dealer in real estate. The Gugenheim family moved out sometime between 1935 and 1936, and by 1940 Albert and Gladys had settled in Amarillo. He continued to be a machinery salesman.

By 1938 Carl A. and Mildred Trautschold had moved in. Carl had just been made president of the C. M. Trautschold Company, which made and/or marketed sashes and doors, stairs, moldings, glass, screens and screen doors, and church and lodge furniture. The company had been founded by his father, Charles Martin Trautschold. Born in Bavaria, a strongly Catholic part of Germany, in 1863, Charles came to the United States with his parents in 1873; they settled in Wisconsin, which, like Texas, welcomed many German immigrants. Charles moved to Waco in 1893 and opened his milling business in 1902. His son Carl joined the business in 1914 and married Mildred Shook in 1926.

The family attended St. Mary of the Assumption Catholic Church, and the Trautschold firm made the communion rail, choir rail, and grilles for the new St. Francis on the Brazos Catholic Church, which was completed in November 1932. (For St. Mary and St. Francis, see *Historic Buildings*, 14 and 12.) Both father and son were deeply involved in the Knights of Columbus, which was something of a Catholic alternative to Freemasonry. Charles was one of the founders of the local council, and Pope Pius XII made Carl a knight commander of the Equestrian Order of Saint Sylvester. In 1940 the household included Carl, 40; Mildred, 36; and their two daughters: Carla, 12, was in the sixth grade, and Rose Mary, 9, was a first-grader. The Trautschold family could also afford a maid, who lived in the garage apartment. In 1940 this was 19-year-old Viola Grappels, a native Texan. ◾

198. William and Lenora Duffel House

1809 Colcord Avenue / 1924–25

Sometimes small houses come in stylish packages. This house was all dressed up in Tudor Revival style, with flat Gothic arches framing the porch, brackets and half-timbering under the main gables, and a Gothic label above the middle of a trio of windows. The door led directly into the living room, and the wall on the right side had a fireplace framed by bookcases with small windows above—all typical of a bungalow. The front room on the left was also accessible from the front porch and was lit by three windows on the front and one on the side. It could easily have been used as a room for rent. To the rear, adjoining the alley, was a one-car garage. There were no accommodations for a servant.

The original owners were William and Lenora Duffel. William C. Duffel was a maternal grandson of John P. Borden, first commissioner of the Texas General Land Office. William worked as an agent for the Franklin Life Insurance Company. Lenora Weaver, William's second wife, was a native of Mart. After Lenora died in 1937, William married Susie Bradley, who was in the house by the time of the 1939 city directory. He lived until 1948; both he and Lenora were buried in Waco's Rosemound Cemetery.

Across the street at 1900 Colcord Avenue was the house of Richard B. and Mary Maude Stanford, built in 1929. He was an attorney and, in 1930, county judge of McLennan County. The Stanfords were quite active in Columbus Avenue Baptist Church. Their house was a Tudor Revival cottage with red brick, which in recent years has been painted a light gray. ■

198. William and Lenora Duffel House

199. William and Myrtle Eastland House

2122 Colcord Avenue   /   1925–26

William Eastland was an officer of the Texas Sand & Gravel Company, along with his brothers, Lee and Roy. The boys grew up a few blocks away at 1226 N. Eighteenth Street, a house that still stands and seems to be a mash-up between the older Victorian style and the more trendy American Foursquare. Their father, Dr. Doyle Eastland, was a physician in practice with Dr. William Crosthwait, who lived a block away at 1104 N. Eighteenth Street; the proximity to the Provident Hospital at Colcord Avenue and Eighteenth must have been seen as very convenient. (For Doyle Eastland's later house, see 172 in this book.) William Eastland and his wife, Myrtle, had three daughters: Eris, Joyce, and Mary Lee.

This was a brick cottage with informal massing and a brick veneer. The bricks were all beige, tan, or light brown; the variance provided a lively character to the walls. Helen Pool of the *News-Tribune* staff commented that it had "a microscopic front porch where you enter the door—and then a great big roomy side porch to make up for the deficiency." To the right was the living room, which Pool noted had a "gray rug, gray walls, gray furniture, and pretty ivory mantel"—the fireplace was against the front wall. Behind the living room was the dining room, lit by a trio of windows, then the kitchen. At the back were the breakfast room and then a sunroom.

Myrtle Eastland reported that the back rooms were actually the center of activity; there "the children have their toys, clothes, food and sleep." It also contained her sewing machine, on which she attempted to mend her very active daughters' clothing. A long hall provided access to the bedroom of the eldest daughter, Eris, then the master bedroom, then the sunroom. The younger daughters, Joyce and Mary Lee, still slept in their parents' bedroom, but they were destined for their own rooms upstairs. The architect is unknown, but the contractor was J. V. Callan, who agreed to build the house for $11,000. He also built the Fred and Della Winchell and Samuel and Regina Appell houses (see *Historic Homes*, 106; and 179 in this book). ■

199. William and Myrtle Eastland House

200. Henry and Johanna Pochyla House

1214 N. Eighteenth Street / 1926

This brick-veneered house, which is somewhere between a bungalow and a Tudor cottage, appears to be one story from the street but has considerable space above stairs. The pair of gables facing the street could be seen as a typical for a bungalow, except for two things: the Tudor-like trim in the gables, and both gables engage with a taller roof behind, which runs the whole width of the building. The smaller of the two gables marked the entrance, while the larger gable marked the porch. As in a bungalow, there was direct entry into the living room, which had a large front window and a fireplace on the side wall flanked by windows. Behind this was the dining room, which projected beyond the side wall of the front room.

Henry Pochyla grew up in Fayette County, the son of a Czech father and a German mother. (Such marriages were disapproved of by both Czech and German parents, but it happened anyway.) In 1905 Henry moved to West, where he opened a meat market. Soon he met and married Johanna Itschner, a Texas native born to German parents. They lived on Cedar Street in West and had three sons: Benjamin, Alfred, and Herbert. In the latter part of 1920 they moved to Waco, where Henry worked as a real estate agent. His office was in the Amicable Building, now better known as the ALICO (see *Historic Buildings*, 55).

They hired Herman F. Cason to design their new house in May 1926. Cason lived just down the block in the house of his parents. He had been a draftsman with T. Brooks Pearson and then with Pearson and Milton W. Scott and later teamed up another Scott draftsman, E. McIver Ross, as Ross & Cason. He also designed St. John's Methodist Church, with his younger brother Harry, in the brief-lived form of Cason Brothers (see *Historic Buildings*, 6). At various times his offices were in the Praetorian Building on Franklin Avenue and the Cameron Building on Austin Avenue (see *Historic Buildings*, 57 and 22). His father, Joseph F. Cason, was a well-known Waco contractor and may well have built this house.

Cason was hired to design a seven-room house to cost $7,500. In 1930 Pochyla informed the census taker that it was worth $12,000, which was a considerable appreciation in just four years. The family did not stay in the house long: by 1935 the Pochylas were living in rural McLennan County, though by 1940 they were back in Waco. In that year Henry was working as the assistant market master for the City of Waco, and Henry, Johanna, and their two youngest children were living at 1708 Proctor, a smaller bungalow that no longer exists. The Cason house stood on its original site into the twenty-first century, but it was purchased and moved out of town.

200. Henry and Johanna Pochyla House

2326 Colcord Avenue   /   1929-30

This house was built for Michael S. Hunt and his wife, Ellen. Michael was a native of what was then the Free State of Ireland—now the Republic of Ireland—and he immigrated to the United States in 1906. He married Ellen Garrity, whose father was also Irish and whose mother was a native Texan, around 1917. He was 33 when they married, and she was 32; a son, Michael Jr., soon came along. They lived first in Corsicana, then Marlin, and moved to Waco in 1925. While in Corsicana Michael founded the Family Life Insurance Company of Texas, and he moved his business to Waco.

As was typical of emigrants from the Republic of Ireland, they were Roman Catholics. In Waco they were members of St. Mary of the Assumption Catholic Church, which was then at Washington Avenue and Ninth in a Gothic revival structure designed by an architect who was also an Irish immigrant—Nicholas J. Clayton of Galveston. Michael was a member of the Knights of Columbus—the Catholic alternative to Freemasonry—and Ellen was president of a women's group, the Catholic Study Club, in 1933-34. She also served on the executive board of the Waco Art League. Michael Jr. attended Waco High, graduating in 1934, and, befitting a good Catholic boy, went on to the University of Notre Dame. When the United States entered World War II, he joined the US Marines and fought for the entire four and a half years of American involvement in the conflict. He then returned to Waco and worked in his father's insurance company.

In Waco the family first lived in a bungalow at 2626 Homan, which is still standing. However, they dreamed of something grander and acquired a corner lot on Colcord Avenue, not far from

201. Michael and Ellen
Hunt House

their first house but on a much more well-to-do street. In July 1929 they were talking with the architect Herman F. Cason about plans for their new house, which they anticipated would cost $17,000. Cason was the son of Waco contractor Joseph F. Cason and learned his design skills in the office of Milton W. Scott and T. Brooks Pearson. In September of that year the contract was awarded to Horace A. Bruyere. While not the busiest Waco contractor, Bruyere had built the Terrell house at 1919 Bosque Boulevard, designed by James P. Baugh; the Clement-Potts house at 2900 Bosque; and the Ralph and Betty McLendon house at 2920 Austin Avenue, both by Birch D. Easterwood. (For these houses, see *Historic Homes*, 94, 85, and 69.)

The move-in date for this house is unusually precise because the Hunts were double-counted in the 1930 US Census. The census taker spoke to Ellen Hunt at their old residence on April 3 and to Michael Hunt in the new house on April 10. The house was essentially a one-story cottage, but the three dormer windows attested to much usable space underneath the roof. The asymmetry of the design suggested something of the earlier Victorian style, but all of the details were Colonial Revival. The most prominent part of the façade was the bay that projected on the right side, and it was lit by a Palladian window, a central window with a semicircular window flanked by a narrower one to each side. To the left was the front porch, with squarish box columns supporting an arcade, which was somewhat suggestive of the early Neoclassical (that is, Federal) style, as was the front door—double doors, actually—with side lights and an elliptical arch above. On the Twenty-Fourth Street side was a porte cochere, with box columns and arches matching those on the front porch. From the porte cochere one stepped into a tiny porch set back from the main wall, which had double French doors opening into the front room.

Inside, the theme of elliptical arches continued, framing double French doors into both front rooms. In between these two rooms was a highly unusual staircase. Set within another elliptical arch, the stair turned to the left, then led to a landing about four feet above the floor. The stairs continued to the right up to the second floor but also stepped down to the rear rooms of the house. The right front room was the largest in the house, with a neoclassical fireplace in the side wall. Windows were placed on the front and both side walls, and a pair of French doors led to the porte cochere, which allowed for excellent circulation in an age before air conditioning. This was certainly intended for entertaining the members of the various groups to which the Hunts belonged. A smaller, less formal living room was on the left, beyond which were the dining room and then a breakfast room.

Curiously, the kitchen was placed in the middle of the house so that it had no windows. This lack of circulation would have certainly made it stiflingly hot during the Waco summers. The Hunts may have been less concerned about that given that they usually hired a cook. Often their cook worked here and lived elsewhere, but in 1932 Minnie Clark was living in an apartment adjoining the garage, and in 1936 Ida Lyons was living there.

Michael Hunt died in 1964, and Michael Jr. became chairman of the board of their insurance company. Michael and his wife lived in Lake Air at 4806 Swan Lake; they attended St. Louis Catholic Church, the newer parish that opened in 1968. Michael Jr. died in 1974, and his mother, in 1975. Both generations of Hunts are buried in Holy Cross Cemetery, the Catholic sacred grounds adjacent to secular Oakwood Cemetery. ◼

202. Jesse and Jewel Lancaster House
(Lancaster-Cunningham-Nathan House)

3505 Carondolet Boulevard   /   Circa 1930

This Tudor Revival cottage had one main floor but considerable room in the attic. A tall gable facing the street sheltered a small front porch; its round-arched opening led to a round-arched front door, which featured imitation strap hinges. Just to the left of this porch was a chimney, marking that the room behind it was to be the living room. This left front room had pairs of windows on the front and side, a modern, non-Tudor touch. The right front room had a trio of windows on the front wall. On the roof were two dormers, large enough to have paired windows.

The original owners were Jesse Lancaster and his wife, Jewel, but they stayed only a few years. Jesse was the manager of the Unclaimed Freight House. The house was vacant in 1934 and in 1936 was occupied by Wade Cunningham and his wife, Eula Frances. Wade was the district freight and passenger agent for the Southern Pacific Railroad. Their stay was even shorter than the Lancasters' because in 1938 the owners were Randolph and Amelia Nathan. However, Randolph died in February 1939 and was buried in Hebrew Rest Cemetery. In 1940 Amelia was living with her 15-year-old daughter, Carol, who was a sophomore in high school, and their live-in butler, Johnny Reed. Amelia estimated the value of their house at $10,000, less than half the value of many of the two-story houses in Castle Heights. ■

202. Jesse and Jewel Lancaster House (Lancaster-Cunningham-Nathan House)

203. Graves and Alice Darby House

503 Carondolet Boulevard   /   Circa 1935–39

In May 1935 the Reverend Graves Darby and his wife, Alice, selected contractor N. A. Palmer to build them a one-story, seven-room house. Palmer had been working in Waco since 1925, when he remodeled the house of Governor Pat Neff on Austin Avenue; he went on to build the Patton house on Colcord Avenue, designed by Birch D. Easterwood, and the Addison Baker and Frances Duncan house and the Lanning-Stevens house in Castle Heights. (For these houses, see *Historic Homes*, 64 and 109; and 189 in this volume.)

The initial plan was for a frame house covered in stucco to be built for $12,000, but as built, the house had a brick veneer and in 1940 had an estimated value of $15,000. Perhaps the change in material caused changes in the process—for whatever reason, Graves and Alice did not move in until late 1938 or early 1939. Graves told the census taker in 1940 that his occupation was preacher or evangelist. Graves was 50, and Alice 47, and they were both highly educated, with six years of education beyond high school.

Like the Lancaster-Cunningham-Nathan house next door, the Darby house had a steeply pitched roof but was much more sculptural. On the left side a gable facing the street wrapped around that end, and on the right side a hipped roof did the same thing; beneath the hipped roof was an open porch. The round-arched door was in a centered gable; to the left were paired windows and to the right, a chimney and another pair of windows. The front door and left window were boldly outlined with quoins and a keystone. The right front window was unadorned, but the porch at the right front corner sported an arcade supported by Doric columns. The overall effect was both picturesque and eclectic. ◼

203. Graves and Alice Darby House

204. John and London Bashara House

2927 Bosque Boulevard   /   1937–38

John Bashara was one of three children of Farris and Francis Bashara, all natives of Syria who immigrated to the United States in 1899. They were living in Waco by 1907, when Farris had established a drugstore. Their native tongue was Assyrian, but they assured the census taker in 1910 that they all spoke English. Initially they lived at 511 N. Sixth Street, a block characterized by shotgun houses and enlarged versions of the shotgun form. By 1910 their store was still on North Sixth, but they were renting a house at 817 S. Eleventh, which would be at the corner of Cleveland, near the northeast corner of the present Kate Ross Apartments. John's parents moved to the south side of town as well, living in a house at 1106 S. Fourth. However, they moved to a newly built bungalow at 3202 Colcord around 1922.

The census records of 1920 showed that John was now married to London Koury (also spelled Khoury), a native of Louisiana whose parents were both from Syria. The household also included his widowed mother and his brother Abe. John gave his occupation as confectioner and reported that he owned a candy store—this was on the south side of the town square. In 1930 John and London were still renting the house at 817; the only other member of the household was their 8-year-old daughter, Elsie. By 1936 the candy store had morphed into the Palace Drug Store, still on the south side of the Square.

John and London moved into this house around 1937 or 1938. In 1940 the census was told that John was 52 and London was 37. Elise was now 18. The household was rounded out by London's older sister, Marie Mitrey, who was a widow at 39, and by her daughter, Marjorie, age 10, who had been born in Indiana. Though John was still running the Palace Drug Store, he told the census taker that he was a confectioner, perhaps suggesting that candies were his true calling.

The house they built was a typical cottage of the 1930s with some aspiration to the Colonial Revival. The main roofline ran from side to side—that is, east to west. The entrance was in a central projecting gable, with direct entry into the living room. A spacious porch, still under the main roof, occupied the left front corner. The brick was a demure light beige; the trim tended to the Colonial Revival. The main ornament feature was the door frame, which had pilasters and a broken triangular pediment over the door. ◼

204. John and London Bashara House

Later Alternatives

205. Ira W. and Martha Seley House
(Braswell-Seley House)

3505 Castle Avenue / 1941–42

This house was doubly tied up with the arrival of a Coca-Cola bottling plant in Waco. The Coca-Cola company sent one of its Georgia employees (and Georgia native), Robert S. Braswell Jr., to build and manage the plant (see *Historic Buildings*, 53). Because the streamlined modern building was designed by a Los Angeles architect, Robert V. Derrah, it was necessary to hire a local architect to oversee the work. T. Brooks Pearson, whose office was just across Eleventh Street, was retained. Work on the plant was started in 1938 and completed in 1939.

Braswell may well have been delighted to find a fellow Georgia native working right across the street, especially since they were to work closely on the construction of the Coca-Cola building. Though Pearson was seventeen years older than Braswell, they both had children who were approaching college age, and Mary Frances Pearson, Carolyn Braswell, and Robert S. Braswell III all studied at the University of Texas in Austin. Though there is no documentation of the architect of this house or the date of construction, it seems highly likely that Pearson designed it for Robert and Mildred Braswell.

In 1941 there were no houses in the 3500 block of what was then Castle Drive, and this was the first house to be built—it was the only house on the block when it was listed in the 1943 city directory. It was not a large house, though more rooms were added much later. The front was two stories, with a brick veneer on the first floor and wooden covering on the second: board-and-batten on the front and weatherboards elsewhere. Underneath the main roof a floor projects out from the wall, with no columns below. Such a cantilevered porch was linked with the Monterrey style from California, though no other details link the house to that style. To the right of the two-story block was an attached garage, certainly one of the first in Waco.

Directly inside the front door was the living room. This room was well lit by a trio of large south-facing windows on the front wall and one on each side of the fireplace on the west side wall. Fireplaces are usually a focal point, but this one has to fight for attention with the staircase that rises across the back wall. The mantel of the fireplace is Georgian (that is, late Colonial Revival), while the delicate balusters seem neoclassical. And as if the room was not busy enough, a round-arched door at the foot of the stairs led into the dining room.

205. Ira W. and Martha Seley House (Braswell-Seley House)

The dining room and the adjoining kitchen were in the single-story part of the house. Windows on the west and north walls provided natural light, while corner cupboards at the northwest and northeast corners provided more Colonial Revival stylings. A semi-octagonal breakfast room just north of the galley kitchen is so consistent with the rest of the rooms that it takes a Sanborn Map to prove that it was added sometime after 1950.

The Braswell family lived in the house only a few years—apparently World War II took them away from Waco for several years. In 1945 it was occupied by Roy J. McKnight and his wife, Bertha; Roy was the business manager at Baylor University. The next year the family had moved to 1807 Lyle, and 3505 Castle was occupied by John and Aleen Shewmake. They were recent arrivals to Waco and did not stay long; John was the manager (and later vice president) of the Southwestern Electric Service.

By April 1950 this became the home of Ira W. Seley; his wife, Martha; and their 3-year-old daughter, Sara. Ira W. Seley, who went by his middle name, Winthrop—"Wimp" to his friends— had serious Waco roots. His grandfather, W. W. Seley, was a prominent banker. (For the arts and crafts house of his aunt, Willie Camille Seley Richey, see 150 in this book.) Winthrop attended

Baylor for his undergraduate degree and then for law school—similarly his uncle, Harvey Richey, had earned a bachelor's degree and a law degree, but at the University of Texas. Winthrop Seley practiced law early and late in his career but spent the years from 1953 to 1961 as vice president of the National City Bank of Waco.

Winthrop was deeply involved in public service. He served on the State Board of Education, as treasurer of the Waco Chamber of Commerce, and on the Waco City Council. He was a director of the Heart of Texas Boy Scouts Council, chairman of the Central Texas March of Dimes, and worked with the Central Texas Red Cross. He was also a Mason and a member of St. Alban's Episcopal Church (see *Historic Buildings*, 16).

In their previous house at 1401 Franklin there had been accommodations out back for servants—in 1940 this was a black couple, John and Elizabeth Washington, but the house on Castle did not have space for servants. Whatever help Martha Seley had worked for wages only.

Winthrop and Martha's only daughter, Sara, married Charles A. Jones, a graduate of University High School of Baylor, who worked as a development officer at Baylor for thirty years. They lived a couple of blocks west of her parents at 3721 Herwol. ◼

206. Dr. Maurice C. and Lavonia Jenkins Barnes House

3217 Robin Road   /   1947–48

Although the end of World War II ushered in an era of modernity to the United States, some Wacoans were quite comfortable with the tried-and-true Colonial Revival, and especially the Southern Colonial Revival. One Waco couple, Dr. Maurice Barnes and his wife, Lavonia Jenkins Barnes, known as "Bobbie," built this house in 1947–48. Dr. Barnes was a graduate of the University of Texas Medical Branch in Galveston (which was the oldest and leading medical school in the state), while Bobbie attended Baylor, with a year at Southern Methodist University.

Maurice and Bobbie had lived in a Foursquare at 2220 Gorman for a couple of years (see 153 in this book), but then lived for a couple of years around 1940 in New York City. Bobbie spent much of her time at the Metropolitan Museum of Art, where the American Wing, which opened in 1924, probably fueled her love of American antiques. She took advantage of continuing education courses, which often included visits to historic house museums in the area. They returned to Waco at the start of World War II.

In 1947 they decided to build their Southern Colonial dream house. The site, on Robin Road, was considered a part of Cameron Park, but the City of Waco was apparently comfortable with selling land farthest from the river if nice houses were to be built. Within a few years another nearby lot on Baker Lane became the home of Waco philanthropist Nell Pape, whose house reflected a specifically Louisiana form of neoclassicism. Lavonia Barnes recalled in 1978 that she had drawn plans for their future home while she and Maurice were living in New York City in 1940. By this she probably meant that she had drawn plans of the arrangement of rooms and specific features; it is doubtful that her drawings were so professional as to be used by a builder without further detailed drawings and specifications.

In those years just before the United States entered the war, she could not have anticipated that she and Maurice would be using elements from an old Waco home when they were building their own home. This was the two-story brick house of Dr. Gregor McGregor and Annie Portia (Fordtran) McGregor at the corner of Columbus Avenue and Eighth Street. The McGregors had previously lived in the hamlet of Wesley in Washington County (their circa 1860 house was moved in 1967 to the Winedale Historical Center near Round Top and restored), and the family moved to Waco in 1873. The house was occupied by two generations of McGregors but was demolished in 1946 to make way for the Masonic Grand Lodge Memorial Temple of Texas (see *Historic Buildings*, 88). Not only the Barnes house but also the house of their neighbors, Irwin and Mary (Barrett) Olsen at 2929 Robin, incorporated features from the McGregor house, including the sandy-pink Waco brick, doors, windows, and other elements. A third house, at 3607 N. Thirty-First, used the cast-iron fence and a latticed well house.

The Barnes house was discussed in great detail on the society page of the *Waco Tribune-Herald* soon after the family moved in. The house was approached on an angle so that visitors could appreciate the way in which it was framed by a backdrop of tall trees. Four white Ionic columns, two stories tall, supported the front portico. The *Tribune* noted that the door, windows, and shutters all came from the McGregor house. In addition, Lavonia Barnes repurposed an old iron fence that she had acquired to become the railing of the balcony over the front door.

Inside, a central stair hall led to the spacious front rooms, the living room and dining room. All these spaces were painted a soft shade of aqua-blue. Also on the first floor were the kitchen, a service pantry, and a powder room. The kitchen had a "dining bay" with large casement windows above pine paneling. This room also had a large fireplace built from old materials; "the only modern touches," opined the *Tribune*, were "the gleaming white stove and the refrigerator." Upstairs were the master bedroom; a bedroom for their son, Warner; and a guest bedroom. Warner's room had pine paneling and calico curtains; it shared a bathroom with the guest bedroom, but both Maurice and Bobbie had their own bathroom, each with its own closet. The basement was not yet finished, but a play room, maid's room, and laundry were planned.

The rooms were furnished with Lavonia Barnes's collection of early-American antiques. In Waco she joined the Heritage Society (which morphed into the Historic Waco Foundation) and authored the books *The Cotton Palace* and *Early Homes of Waco*. She worked closely with Raiford Stripling, who was emerging as the dean of Texas restoration architects on such projects as the Earle-Harrison house (see *Historic Homes*, 3) and East Terrace (see *Historic Homes*, 8). Stripling wrote the foreword to *Early Homes of Waco* and called Lavonia Barnes "one of the stalwart leaders and an indefatigable worker in the Waco preservation and restoration program." ◼

206. Dr. Maurice C. and Lavonia Jenkins Barnes House

207. Mrs. Hattie Richards House

3706 Chateau Avenue   /   1949–50

In the summer of 1949 interior designer Allan Richards hired Dallas architects Roscoe DeWitt and Arch B. Swank to design a house for his mother, Hattie, in Castle Heights. Hattie was the widow of Ben C. Richards, longtime proprietor of the Waco Fish Market and a one-time mayor of Waco who died in March 1949.

Both DeWitt and Swank had practiced architecture in Dallas for close to two decades. Roscoe DeWitt was a native of Dallas who attended Dartmouth College and Harvard University for his master of arts in architecture; his work before the war included the design of the Dallas Museum of Fine Arts in Fair Park. Arch Swank, also a Texan, was a graduate of Texas A&M University; in the 1930s he had been the partner of O'Neil Ford, and together they designed houses in Denton, Dallas, and San Antonio, as well as a thoroughly modern ranch house on St. Joseph Island for Texas oilman Sid Richardson. In their house designs Ford and Swank attempted to meld the Prairie progressivism of Frank Lloyd Wright, the modern materials of the International style, and the rugged simplicity of early-Texas vernacular houses. They also designed the Little Chapel in the Woods at what is now Texas Woman's University in Denton. Both DeWitt and Swank served in World War II, DeWitt as one of the "Monuments Men" who retrieved vast amounts of art that had been stolen by the Nazis.

In a neighborhood devoted to traditional styles, this house pointed in a more modern direction. The house had brick walls with generously scaled windows and was covered by two interlocking hipped roofs. The entrance was not in front but at the angle of the L-shaped front porch. This porch was supported by cast-iron pilasters in a wrought-iron frame. A chimney projected out from the east side wall and rose through the front hipped roof. The house was low key, with a restrained use of ornament and a concern for spacious and light-filled rooms.

The entrance was to the left of the chimney and opened into a shallow foyer. The living room was to the right, and two bedrooms, to the left. In the living room the fireplace was on the near side wall, with a simple neoclassical mantelpiece; it faced a bay window with a large plate-glass window on the opposite side wall. The house had many modern features, including Formica countertops in the kitchen and one of the earliest air-conditioning systems in a Waco house. All floors were carpet over plywood, except for linoleum in the kitchen and breakfast room and a rubber tile floor in the two bathrooms. Out back was a one-car garage with a small apartment for a servant. ◼

207. Mrs. Hattie Richards House

208. George and Adele Bashara House

3201 Colcord Avenue   /   Circa 1951

This house, along with the bungalow across the street built three decades earlier, represents two generations of a Waco family that emigrated from the Middle East, variously described as Syrian or Lebanese. In 1900 the matriarch of the family, Nora Bashara, was living in Waco with her sons Farris and Mansoor, daughter Sadie, and two nieces. Mansoor moved to Beaumont and then to Wichita Falls, where he prospered in the oil business. Farris became a wholesale dealer in wood, while his younger brother Samuel, drawing on his Middle Eastern heritage, sold what was called either silk goods or oriental goods. From 1907 to 1916 they lived at 511 N. Sixth, the largest house on a block with many shotgun houses. In 1917 they moved to 1101 S. Fourth, but by 1921 they were building the house at 3202 Colcord. The house was on the edge of the prairie and the only thing for blocks—perhaps they got a good price on the lot for serving as suburban pioneers.

In 1922, when they were newly settled in the house, there were two couples in residence: Farris and his wife, Sarah; and their son George and his new bride, Adele (Sotel) Bashara, who were both 23. Before the end of 1922 the family was joined by a daughter, Vivian; sons George Jr. and Edward were to follow. Farris continued to sell wood—in one census he explained that he was a fuel dealer—while George was a farmer, presumably growing much of the family's food. By 1940 he had become a building contractor.

The house at 3202 Colcord was a low-slung bungalow. While many Wacoans were abandoning this style for various period houses, many Arts and Crafts style houses were still being built. Indeed, Wacoans had still been building late-Victorian houses in the first decade of the twentieth century. Most of the house is under a single roofline running from the front gable to the back; another gable, facing Thirty-Second Street, shelters the porch that wraps around to that side. (An unfortunate later addition blocked the south side of the porch.) Typical bungalow features are the brackets supporting the eaves and the pairing of windows. A lesser-used bungalow feature is the railing of the front porch, which is a low brick wall rather than consisting of balusters. The paired windows in the front back and side gables suggest that there was much usable room in the attic, either as storage or living space.

In 1940 the household still consisted of Farris and Sarah, George and Adele, and their three (now teenage) kids. The house, which they had valued at $8,000 in 1930, was now valued at half that, thanks to ten years of the Great Depression. However, they were able to afford a maid who lived at the rear. Renting for six dollars a month were two African American women. They were both maids, but apparently one worked elsewhere. Gertrude Manning, 26, was head of that household, and Annie Mae Philips, 25, was listed in the census as her partner. (This may have been a business term rather than a relationship term.) These women had educational attainments similar to those of the folks who occupied the front of the house: Gertrude attended two years of high school, and Annie Mae completed one year of college. Their move to Waco was recent, as five years earlier Gertrude had been living in Freestone County, and Annie Mae in Williamson County.

World War II impacted all three Bashara children in various ways. Vivian attended a USO dance in Waco and met the man of her dreams, Robert Theodore Weisberg, of Brooklyn, New

208. George and Adele Bashara House

York. He was just about to be shipped out, but he and Vivian married after the war. George attended the University of Texas and then served in the army air corps during the war; Edward attended Texas A&M University and then served in the army. When Edward came home from the war, he joined his father in the construction business. The house at 3201 Colcord is one that they built.

The house almost looked like a villa built somewhere along the shores of the Mediterranean: stone walls, a red tile roof, plenty of porches and windows. The first floor was a veneer of Texas limestone, which was just becoming popular as a material for modern Texas houses, while the upper floor was a buff-colored brick. The windows were modern casements with metal frames, a type that had first appeared in Waco in the early 1930s in the Kestner, Duncan, and Tanenbaum houses in Castle Heights (see *Historic Homes*, 110 and 109; and 190 in this volume). A circular window to the left of the door was filled with colored glass; beneath this was the mail drop. The current awnings are not the original ones, but this feature was immensely popular in twentieth-century Texas before air conditioning came into wide use. On the upper floor and some lower-floor windows were small iron balconies that could hold flowers. Planted in front of the house are cedars of Lebanon, an unusual choice for a Waco front yard but one that was perfectly logical for a family with proud Lebanese roots.

The house does not seem large from the outside but has many rooms inside, albeit relatively small ones. The front door led into a stair hall, with an iron balustrade on the left wall. Through an arched opening was the living room, directly ahead was the dining room, and to the left were two additional rooms. The living room was lit by large windows on the front and east side wall, and on the longer back wall was a fireplace encased in the same limestone as the front of the house. Beyond this to the east was a sunroom with a concrete floor, which also had modern casement windows. A short stair just behind the sunroom provided secondary access both into the living room and a passage behind it, which connected with the stair hall. To the left of the stair hall was a one-story wing with two rooms, the front one perhaps an office or sitting room, the one behind it a bedroom.

Upstairs were three bedrooms and one large bathroom, perhaps originally two, as there were doors from the hallway and the master bedroom. The master bedroom was at the northeast corner and had a door onto a deck above the sunroom. In the small upper hall, there was an attic fan, which kept air moving on hot Texas nights. Just inside that door was a laundry chute that sent dirty clothes and sheets to the laundry in the basement; a chute in the kitchen closet did the same for dirty towels. The house also had a full basement, lit on the west side by windows just above the grade. ◼

   Chapter Seven

209. Charles K. and Katherine Durham House (Durham-Buchanan-Morrow House)

2200 Colcord Avenue / Circa 1922–23, remodeled 1966

When driving by this house, prepare to be confused. There are several Victorian features, including stained glass and a bay window, but also prominent forward-facing gables, as if it were a bungalow. It sits on a large lot, which is the original size—there was no house that once sat in the west side yard—and there is a large Victorian gazebo. The ensemble was the idiosyncratic statement of a Waco educator, Eb Morrow.

The house was built for Charles K. Durham and his wife, Katherine (Renfro) Durham, around 1922. (Sometimes the house is dated 1916; the street address does not show up in the city directories until 1923–24.) Charles had a loan business that operated out of the ALICO Building. Katherine was the daughter of Thomas I. and Susan Renfro, the second owners of the Wright-Renfro house at 601 Dallas in East Waco (see *Historic Homes*, 28). Charles and Katherine had one son, Charles, and two daughters, Lucille and Allene. Lucille married John H. Nash, who had grown up in the Victorian mansion of his parents, Elihu and Fanny Nash, at 1703 Sanger (see *Historic Homes*, 15), and as a young man worked in his father's lumber business. Early in their marriage they lived with Lucille's parents, but when Charles and Kate moved into this

209. Charles K. and Katherine Durham House (Durham-Buchanan-Morrow House)

house, John and Lucille settled into a snug bungalow at 2310 Morrow. Younger daughter Allene attended Baylor, then taught school in Stephenville, but in 1926 married Reed Compton, a local boy and graduate of Texas A&M University. By 1930 the Durham nest was empty: the household was Charles, Kate, and their cook, Ella Scruggs, a 35-year-old divorced African American woman.

In the late 1930s the house had a new owner: Mrs. Robert (Ella Catherine) Buchanan, formerly of Stamps, Arkansas. She was 62 and a widow in 1940. Her decision to live in this house was strictly familial: across Colcord at 2201 was her daughter Omah, now Mrs. Roy Albaugh, and across Twenty-Second Street was her daughter Mary, now Mrs. Dees McDermott (see *Historic Homes*, 75 and 98). Her granddaughter, Mary Dees McDermott, was 15 in 1940, and after World War II she married Herbert L. Hicks, a jet pilot who served at Bryan Air Force Base just west of College Station. After his discharge from the air force they lived in this house for a while, then moved to Colorado Springs so that Herbert could pursue business opportunities. After Ella Buchanan passed away, the estate rented the house to officers at Blackland Air Field, which was where St. Louis Catholic Church now stands. Most notable were General and Mrs. Bruce K. Holloway, who lived here in the late 1950s.

All this time the house was a simple bungalow, with a rectangular footprint and a porch across the front that partially wrapped around the Twenty-Second Street side. Out back was a one-car garage. When E. B. "Eb" Morrow, the longtime Waco educator, bought the house, some changes were made—to put it mildly. Eb was much involved in the Historic Waco Foundation, and in 1973 he attended the Attingham Summer School, which studies the English country house in its social context. He acquired parts of the soon-to-be-demolished Lyons-Adelman house on North Fifth Street near Waco Drive and from the W. W. Cameron house on Austin Avenue, both designed by W. W. Larmour. Eb then hired Robert Braswell of Braswell-Davis and Associates, architects and interior designers, to incorporate the old parts in a remodeling of the house.

Originally Eb wanted to cover the house with black-gray asbestos siding, which he had seen on a house on Cumberland Avenue. Braswell, whom Eb knew as Bobby, pointed out that the overall effect might be too much and suggested that the main façade be covered with light gray Crown bricks. These bricks were used to enclose the porch on the front and the east side. Where the side porch stopped, they built a porte cochere with slender cast-iron posts. On the right part of the front they reused a Victorian bay window.

Braswell and Morrow created a new entrance hall by enclosing the front part of the old porch. Beyond this was a central room, in which they framed a fireplace with rectangular wooden panels, presumably from one of the Larmour houses. Beyond this fireplace was a long room created by enclosing the side porch; it had a door at the back, filled with repurposed stained glass, leading out onto the porte cochere. Behind the central room was the dining room, lit by three windows facing Twenty-Second Street; on its back wall was the main staircase in the house. A door on the left led into the kitchen. The large master bedroom was on the west side, with its space enlarged by a bay window from one of the Larmour houses.

There was usable room in the attic, and at the back Eb create a guest suite. The balustrade of the upper stair hall was made of balusters from one of the jury boxes of the McLennan County Courthouse of 1900–02 by J. Riely Gordon. Apparently, these nicely turned balusters became available when one of the courtrooms was remodeled in a drearily modern style.

Eb also acquired the turret at the top of the tower of the Lyons house, which he placed in his side yard to serve as a gazebo or summer house. The structure did not have an interior originally, so Eb decorated the inside with brackets from the front porch of a house near Waxahachie.

The house was featured on the heritage tour known as "Pilgrimage to Historical Waco" in April 1967, along with East Terrace, the Fort House, the Earle-Napier Kinnard house (all houses destined to be part of Historic Waco), and the Waco Garden Center at 1705 N. Fifth—also known as the Johnson-Taylor house (see 170 in this book). Since Eb's death in 2003 the house has had a couple of owners; the gazebo remains a local landmark. ◼

MORE ARCHITECTS OF WACO HOUSES

Roy E. Lane (attributed)

150. Harvey Mac and Willie
Richey House
1825 Colonial Avenue
Circa 1915

Milton W. Scott

154. Crawford Apartments
(later Austin Place)
2000 Austin Avenue
1916

156. Terrace Court (later Terrace
Gardens) Apartments
611–617 N. Fourth Street
1916–17

Birch D. Easterwood

174. J. Luther and Mae Staton House
(Staton-Dumas House)
2524 Austin Avenue
1922–23

175. Coleman and Stella
Kendrick House
2801 Maple Avenue
1923–24

177. Valentine and Kathleen Cox
House (Nabors-Cox House)
2925 Maple Avenue
1925

182. Carl and Elsie Wallerstedt House
201 N. Thirty-Eighth Street
1933

186. Walter and Ida King House
2305 Morrow Avenue
1923
(as Easterwood & King)

188. J. Bruton and Frances
Orand House
3415 Chateau Avenue
1925–26

192. George and Lillie Liddell House
2800 Maple Avenue
1933–34

James P. Baugh

176. Harry T. Cruger House
3025 Maple Avenue
1924

E. McIver Ross

179. Charles Samuel and Regina
Appell House
909 N. Eighteenth Street
1925–26

Herman F. Cason

185. T. Walter and Eula
Harrell House
3625 Castle Avenue
1938–39

196. Herman and Carrie
Cason House
2900 Columbus Avenue
1941

200. Henry and Johanna
Pochyla House
1214 N. Eighteenth Street
1926

201. Michael and Ellen Hunt House
2326 Colcord Avenue
1929–30

T. Brooks Pearson

195. Harry and Sadie Kestner House
3601 Austin Avenue
1935

205. Ira W. and Martha Seley House
(Braswell-Seley House)
3505 Castle Avenue
1941–42

Wilford S. Bogue (Fort Worth)

197. Albert and Esther Gugenheim
House (Gugenheim-Trautschold
House)
2901 Sanger Avenue
1924

DeWitt and Swank (Dallas)

207. Mrs. Hattie Richards House
3706 Chateau Avenue
1949–50

SOURCES

Digital Resources

Waco City Directories from 1876 to 1923–24 are digitized and available online via the Baylor University Libraries Digital Collections at https://digitalcollections-baylor.quartexcollections.com/texas-collection-collections/waco-city-directories-1876–1923.

Sanborn Fire Insurance Maps are available at the Library of Congress at https://www.loc.gov/collections/sanborn-maps/?fa=location:texas%7Clocation:mclennan+county%7Clocation:waco.

Many Texas Sanborn Fire Insurance Maps in Perry-Castañeda Library Map Collection at the University of Texas are available at https://legacy.lib.utexas.edu/maps/sanborn/texas.html.

Many Waco (and Texas) newspapers are digitized and available on the Portal to Texas History at https://texashistory.unt.edu/.

United States Census Records up to 1940 have been digitized and are accessible through Heritage Quest Online, as part of Ancestry.com.

Sources for the historical information in the text are listed by house on the following pages.
Frequently cited sources have been shortened as indicated below:

Du Bois, "The Waco Horror" — W. E. B. Du Bois (based on reporting by Elisabeth Freeman), "The Waco Horror," *The Crisis* 12, no. 3 (July 1916, supplement): 1–8.

Greaves and Walker, *Milton W. Scott's Waco* — B. J. Greaves and Mildred G. Walker, *Milton W. Scott's Waco* (Waco: Dr Pepper Museum and Free Enterprise Institute, 1998).

Kelley, *The Handbook of Waco* — Dayton Kelley, ed., *The Handbook of Waco and McLennan County, Texas* (Waco: Texian Press, 1972).

Larmour, *Architectural Waco* — W. W. Larmour, *Architectural Waco: Showing Principal Buildings Erected by W. W. Larmour, Architect* (Waco: Brooks and Wallace, n.d. [circa 1896]); reprinted in *Waco Heritage and History* 4, no. 3 (Fall 1973): 1–22.

TGCAMB — *Texas General Contractors Association Monthly Bulletin* [accessed at the Metropolitan Research Center, Houston Public Library].

Wallace, *A Spirit So Rare* — Patricia Ward Wallace, *A Spirit So Rare: A History of the Women of Waco* (Austin: Nortex Press, 1984).

WCCN — "Beautiful Waco—a Home and Garden Number," *Waco Chamber of Commerce News*, April–May 1926, reprinted in *Waco Heritage and History* 1, no. 1 (Spring 1970): 26–48.

WCCN II — Undated issue of *Waco Chamber of Commerce News*, reprinted as "Examples of Later Day Waco Homes," *Waco Heritage and History* 6, no. 4 (Winter 1975): 26–36.

Chapter One. Victorian Homes

121. **Meredith and Annie Sullivan House**
Waco City Directories, 1878–79 to 1936
US Census, 1880–1940
Sanborn Map, 1916, sheet 65
Waco News-Tribune, January 31, 1932 (Annie Ola
Sullivan's obituary); April 11, 1956 (Richard M. "Dick"
Sullivan's obituary)
"The Forty Singers," *Waco Heritage and History* 4, no. 3
(Fall 1973): 23–40 (reprint of 1906 program and a
one-page 1949 retrospective, no author given)

122. **Fred and Marie Koos House**
Waco City Directories, 1886–87 to 1923–24
US Census, 1900–1930
Sanborn Maps, 1899, sheet 46; 1926, sheet 23
Waco News-Tribune, October 14, 1954 (Marie Koos's
obituary)

123. **Charles and Maude Hamilton House**
US Census 1900 (Isla David), 1910–1930 (Hamiltons),
and 1940 (Bain and Bell)
Waco City Directories, 1900–01 to 1923–24
Du Bois, "The Waco Horror," 8
Waco Times-Herald, December 16, 1927 (Charles's
obituary)
Sanborn Maps, 1899, sheet 44; 1926, sheet 14; 1926/1950,
sheet 14
Amanda Freudensprung, "New Life for Hamilton
House: 120-Year-Old Building Becomes Home for
Business," *Waco Tribune Herald*, April 25, 2013

124. **Patrick and Nora Cahill House**
Waco City Directories, 1888–89 to 1923–24
Sanborn Maps, 1899, sheet 33; 1926, sheet 33; 1926/1950,
sheet 33
US Census, 1900–1910

125. **Richard and Mary Munroe House**
US Census, 1900, 1910
Waco City Directories, 1882 to 1923–24
Sanborn Maps, 1926, sheet 238; 1926/1950, sheet 238
Waco Morning News, March 25, 1893, 4; April 3, 1893, 5
B. B. Paddock, *A History of Central and Western Texas*
(Chicago: Lewis Publishing, 1911), 1:800–02
(biography of Judge Munroe)
Du Bois, "The Waco Horror," 3–4, 6–8

126. **Joseph and Adeline Perry House**
Sanborn Maps, 1899, sheet 27; 1926, sheet 208; 1926/
1950, sheet 208
US Census, 1900–1940
Waco City Directories, 1894–95 to 1923–24
Waco Times Herald, February 14, 1908 (Joseph Perry's
obituary)

127. **Hardie H. and Bessie M. Holt House**
Waco City Directories, 1894–95 to 1941
US Census, 1900–1930

128. **Edward and Elizabeth Jones House
(Jones-Carothers-Rowell House)**
Waco City Directories, 1896–97 to 1923–24
US Census, 1900–1930
Sanborn Maps, 1899, sheet 43; 1926, sheet 201; 1926/
1950, sheet 201
Waco Times-Herald, September 4, 1900, 5
(Edward's obituary)

129. **James N. and Sarah Harris House**
Waco City Directories, 1876 to 1900–01
US Census, 1900, 1910
Sanborn Map, 1926, sheet 87
J. B. Smith, "Slipping Away: In Search of Waco's
Most Endangered Historic Buildings," *Waco
Tribune-Herald*, April 19, 2015

130. **Victorian Single-Wall Rent House**
Sanborn Maps, 1899, sheet 53; 1926, sheet 84; 1926/1950,
sheet 50
Waco City Directories, 1898–99 to 1923–24
US Census, 1900–1940
Rhiannon Saegert, "Single-Wall Standout: One-of-a-
Kind East Waco Home Gets Historic Landmark
Designation," *Waco Tribune-Herald*, March 13, 2020

131. **John L. Pippin House**
Waco City Directories, 1904–05 to 1941
Sanborn Map, 1926, sheet 77

132. **Wade and Carrie Morrison House
(Morrison-Lanham-Crowder House)**
Waco City Directories, 1884–85 to 1923–24
US Census, 1900–1940
Mike Copeland, "Historic Mansions Hit the Market in
Downtown Waco," *Waco Tribune-Herald*, May 13, 2018

133. **John F. and Addie Rowe House**
Waco City Directories, 1902–03 to 1923–24
US Census, 1910 and 1920 (Waco), 1930 (Dallas)
Sanborn Map, 1926, sheet 202

134. **Pecan Street Shotgun House**
Waco City Directories, 1898–99 to 1923–23
US Census, 1910–1940
Sanborn Maps, 1899, sheet 53; 1926, sheet 84

135. **Jeremiah and Cordelia Early House**
Waco City Directories, 1876 to 1948
US Census, 1880–1940
Sanborn Map, 1926, sheet 230
Houston *Union*, July 6, 1870, quoted in Alwyn Barr
and Robert A. Calvert, eds., *Black Leaders: Texans
for Their Times* (Austin: Texas State Historical
Association, 1981), 76n29 (Richard Allen and the
Morris house)

136. **Thomas and Emma Sterling House**
Waco City Directories, 1898–99 to 1923–24
US Census, 1910, 1920
Sanborn Map, 1926, sheet 222

137. **Sinclair-Sarratt House (later Good
Neighbor Settlement House)**
Waco City Directories, 1878–79 to 1934
US Census, 1910–1930
Sanborn Maps, 1926, sheet 240; 1926/1950, sheet 240
Waco News-Tribune, May 31, 1924, 8 (death of J. D.
Sinclair)
Waco Tribune-Herald, July 31, 1937 (Julia's obituary)
Benjamin Risher Sleeper and Luella Conger Boynton,
*The Windows of St. Paul's Episcopal Church, Waco,
Texas* (booklet in collection of the author), 1
Terri Jo Ryan, "Good Neighbor House Attempts to
Bring Change to the Community," *Waco Tribune
Herald*, June 30, 2012

138. **Cullom-Butler House**
Waco City Directories, 1910–41
US Census, 1880–1940
Sanborn Maps, 1926, sheet 240; 1926/1950, sheet 240
Waco Morning News, February 17, 1912, 2; June 6, 1915, 10

Chapter Two. Bungalows and Foursquares

139. **Rogers-Bexley House**
Waco City Directories, 1907–08 to 1923–24
US Census, 1910–1930
Sanborn Map, 1926, sheet 239
Waco News Tribune, May 7, 1954

140. **William and Jennie Colgin House**
Waco Morning News, February 23, 1912, 7
Waco City Directories, 1882 to 1923–24
US Census, 1900–1940
Sanborn Maps, 1926, vol. II, sheet 339; 1926/1950,
vol. II, sheet 339

141. **Mrs. Mettie Fisher House**
Waco City Directories, 1910–51
Sanborn Maps, 1916, sheet 65; 1926, sheet 306; 1926/
1950, sheet 306
US Census, 1900–1920
Waco Morning News, January 2, 1913, 8

142. **Dave and Jennie Hawtof House**
Waco City Directories, 1910–36
US Census, 1900–1940
Sanborn Maps, 1926, sheet 14; 1926/1950, sheet 14
Waco News-Tribune, February 9, 1933, 3; February 10,
1933, 2 (Dave's obituary and funeral); June 3, 1950, 10
(Emanuel in real estate)

143. **Tom and Mary Bush House**
Waco City Directories, 1910 to 1917–18
US Census, 1910–1940
Sanborn Map, 1926, sheet 14
WCCN, 33
Kelley, *The Handbook of Waco*, 44

144. **Wheatley-Corwin-Kindler House**
Waco City Directories, 1911–12 to 1923–24
US Census, 1900–1940
Sanborn Maps, 1926, sheet 237; 1926/1950, sheet 237

145. **Clyde and Katherine Spencer Webb House
(Webb-Johnson House)**
Waco City Directories, 1910–28
US Census, 1900–1940

Sanborn Maps, 1926, sheet 238; 1926/1950, sheet 238
Waco Morning News, January 19, 1913, 3 (move-in);
    July 21, 1917, 1 (Clyde drafted)
Waco News-Tribune, August 9, 1946 (Jennie's obituary);
    November 14, 1946 (Clyde's obituary); February 13,
    1947 (Kathy's obituary)
Cornerstone, Waco High School
TGCAMB, November 1924, 34; August 1927, 33;
    September 1928, 25; March 1929, 32; May 1929, 32

146. Harry L. and Bertie Spencer House
Waco City Directories, 1911–12 to 1923–24
US Census, 1920, 1930
Sanborn Map, 1926, sheet 238
Waco Morning News, March 26, 1913, 7 (building permit)
Waco News-Tribune, November 4, 1960 (Harry Lee
    Spencer's obituary)

**147. Allan and Frances Sanford House
(Sanford-Barrett House)**
Waco City Directories, 1911–12 to 1923–24
US Census, 1920–1940
Du Bois, "The Waco Horror," 2–3, 8
TGCAMB, June 1925, 25 (Neff remodel)
Sanborn Map, 1926, sheet 339
WCCN, 36 (Neff), 40 (Sanford-Barrett)
Kelley, *The Handbook of Waco*, 238 (Sanford),
    201–02 (Neff)

148. J. Edward and Laura Brown House
Waco City Directories, 1910 to 1923–24
US Census, 1900–1940
Sanborn Maps, 1926, sheet 240; 1926/1950, sheet 240
Waco Morning News, January 8, 1915, 3; April 25, 1915, 8;
    July 17, 1916, 7
Waco News-Tribune, February 19, 1919, 7; July 7, 1920, 5;
    June 15, 1924, 3; February 24, 1927, 6; June 26, 1928, 4;
    October 3, 1928, 7; November 22, 1928, 6; December
    1, 1932, 11; December 11, 1932, 14; December 3, 1933, 15;
    November 6, 1935, 5; January 29, 1936, 5; February 8,
    1938, 5

149. George and Eleanor Perry House
Waco City Directories, 1913–48
US Census, 1910 (Hamilton), 1920–1940 (Waco)
Sanborn Maps, 1926, sheet 289; 1926/1950, sheet 289

150. Harvey Mac and Willie Richey House
Waco City Directories, 1913 to 1923–24
US Census, 1910–1940
Sanborn Maps, 1926, sheet 223; 1926/1950, sheet 223
Photo of drawing of the house in Roy E. Lane Papers,
    Texas Collection, Baylor University
WCCN II, 35

151. Jesse J. and Jessie Dean House
Waco City Directories, 1913–26
Waco Morning News, December 16, 1916, 3
US Census, 1920, 1930
Sanborn Maps, 1926, sheet 294; 1926/1950, sheet 294

152. Milo and Florence Wilkins House
Waco City Directories, 1896–97 to 1926
US Census, 1900–1930
Sanborn Maps, 1926, sheet 72; 1926/1950, sheet 72

153. Weathered-Vick-Barnes House
Waco City Directories, 1913 to 1923–24
US Census, 1920–1940
Sanborn Maps, 1926, sheet 308; 1926/1950, sheet 308

154. Crawford Apartments (later Austin Place)
Waco City Directories, 1916 to 1920–21
US Census, 1920–1940
Sanborn Maps, 1926, sheet 339; 1926/1950, sheet 339
Waco Morning News, December 29, 1915, 8; August 6,
    1916, 25
Waco Tribune-Herald, December 20, 1973 (Crawford's
    obituary)
Wallace, *A Spirit So Rare*, 226–31 (Gus and Nell Pape)
Greaves and Walker, *Milton W. Scott's Waco*, 45

155. Joe and Rose Snaman House
Waco City Directories, 1910 to 1923–24
US Census, 1920–1940
Sanborn Maps, 1916, sheet 65; 1926, sheet 215
WCCN II, 32
Author photographs of the house with porch newly
    demolished, May 19, 2008

156. Terrace Court (later Terrace Gardens) Apartments
McLennan County Deed Records, vol. 282, 478
Waco City Directories, 1904–05 to 1930–31
Waco Morning News, July 1, 1915, 5

Waco News-Tribune, October 7, 1928, 17
US Census, 1930
Sanborn Maps, 1899, sheet 15; 1926, sheet 212; 1926/
1950, sheet 212
Greaves and Walker, *Milton W. Scott's Waco*, 45

157. Howard and Susie Dudgeon House
Waco City Directories, 1913 to 1923–24
US Census, 1920–1940
Sanborn Maps, 1926, sheet 308; 1926/1950, sheet 308

158. Randolph and Gertrude Wilson House
Waco City Directories, 1910–36
US Census, 1910–1940
Sanborn Maps, 1926, sheet 308; 1926/1950, sheet 308
TGCAMB, January 1924, 28; February 1924, 34; March
1924, 20, 34

159. William and Sibyl Glasgow House
Waco City Directories, 1913 to 1923–24
US Census, 1920–1940
Sanborn Maps, 1926, sheet 308; 1926/1950, sheet 308
The West News (West, Texas), November 17, 1933, 1

160. Buford-Fair House
Waco City Directories 1906–07 to 1923–24
Sanborn Maps, 1926, sheet 76; 1926/1950, sheet 76
US Census, 1920, 1930

161. Thomas and Martha Primm House
Waco City Directories, 1894–95 to 1923–24
US Census, 1880, 1900, 1920, 1930
Sanborn Maps, 1926, sheet 294; 1926/1950, sheet 294

162. Dennis and Maggie Dodson House
Waco City Directories, 1916 to 1923–24
Sanborn Maps, 1926, sheet 242; 1926/1950 sheet 242
Waco News-Tribune, March 14, 1926, 20; May 17, 1927, 5
(Oscar's graduation)

163. John M. and Edwina Sturgis Davis House
Waco City Directories, 1911–12 to 1923–24
US Census, 1880–1930
Waco News-Tribune, May 31, 1918, 5 (luncheon for
Dorothy Finlay); October 18, 1921 (Katherine's
obituary); December 1, 1958 (Edwina's obituary)

Sanborn Maps, 1889, sheet 12; 1893, sheet 6; 1899,
sheet 17 (Sturgis house on Fifth); 1926, sheet 236;
1926/1950, sheet 236 (Davis house on Colcord)
Larmour, *Architectural Waco*, 4 and 18

164. Thomas Henry and Nannie Munnerlyn House
Sanborn Map, 1926, sheet 242
Waco City Directories, 1916 to 1923–24
US Census, 1920–1940

165. Louis and Ada Roter House
Waco City Directories, 1916 to 1923–24
US Census, 1930 (Dallas)
Waco News-Tribune, July 3, 1920, 5; July 31, 1921, 28;
October 2, 1921, 12; December 7, 1921, 1; October 7,
1928, 17, March 9, 1929, 15
WCCN ll, 28

166. James and Marie Fadal House
Waco City Directories, 1902–03 to 1936
US Census, 1910–1940
Sanborn Maps, 1899, sheet 50 (house in East Waco);
1926, sheet 72 (store in East Waco); 1926, sheet 235
(house on Lasker)

167. Peach Street Shotgun House
Sanborn Maps, 1899, sheet 52 (empty lots); 1926, sheet
84; 1926/1950, sheet 84
Waco City Directories, 1921–22 to 1941
US Census, 1940

**168. First Presbyterian Manse
(Charles and Millicent Caldwell House)**
Sanborn Maps, 1899, sheet 30 (furnished rooms
and 1004 Austin); 1926, sheet 316 (new house)
Waco City Directories, 1904–05 to 1941
TGCAMB, March 1925, 34
"Dr. and Mrs. C. T. Caldwell Open Manse," *Waco
News-Tribune*, December 1, 1925, 5
Du Bois, "The Waco Horror," 8

169. Jesse and Emma Harrison House
Waco City Directories, 1880–81 to 1945
Sanborn Maps, 1899, sheet 53; 1916, sheet 53; 1926,
sheet 75; 1926/1950, sheet 75
US Census, 1900–1940

Chapter Three. Colonial Revival

170. **Peter and Eva Taylor House**
    (also known as the Johnson-Taylor House)
    Waco City Directories, 1876 to 1923–24
    Waco Morning News, June 12, 1913, 3; February 25, 1915, 3; May 13, 1917, 15
    Waco News-Tribune, August 30, 1924, 9
    Sanborn Maps, 1916, sheet 66 (old Taylor house); 1926, sheet 256; 1926/1950, sheet 256
    WCCN, 28
    Wallace, *A Spirit So Rare*, 257

171. **Elton and Maude Hunter House**
    Waco City Directories 1919–20 to 1939
    US Census, 1930, 1940
    Sanborn Maps, 1926, sheet 308; 1926/1950, sheet 308
    R. J. Tolson, *A History of Wm. Cameron & Co., Inc.* (Waco: J. S. Barnett, circa 1923–25); copy in the Texas Collection, Baylor University

172. **Williamson-Eastland-Woodson House**
    Waco City Directories, 1919–20 to 1941
    US Census, 1920–1940
    Waco News-Tribune, October 17, 1921, 6 (good cook wanted); October 5, 1924, 14 (cook and yard man); October 23, 1924, 13 (residence for sale); January 1, 1925, 15 ("for quick sale"); September 5, 1927, 3 (Cullen F. Thomas); December 23, 1928, 19 (colonial simplicity); January 13, 1929, 1 (Dr. Eastland's obituary)
    Sanborn Maps, 1926, sheet 338; 1926/1950, sheet 338
    Robert Bruce Blake, "Thomas, Cullen Fleming (1868–1938)," *Handbook of Texas Online*, accessed February 9, 2019, http://www.tshaonline.org/handbook/online/articles/ftho6

173. **William and Mary Darden House**
    Waco City Directories, 1921–22 to 1943
    Waco News-Tribune, May 9, 1923, 5; June 1, 1927, 3
    WCCN, 47
    Conversation with Waco historian T. Bradford Willis, July 16, 2018

174. **J. Luther and Mae Staton House**
    (Staton-Dumas House)
    Waco City Directories, 1921–22 to 1941
    US Census, 1910–1940
    TGCAMB, August 1922, 24
    Waco News-Tribune, May 25, 1924, 29 ("Some

Easterwood Landmarks"); December 28, 1924, 1 (James's obituary); May 26, 1926, 5; May 30, 1926, 16; June 17, 1926, 5 (wedding)
    WCCN, 47

175. **Coleman and Stella Kendrick House**
    US Census, 1900–1940
    Waco News-Tribune, May 25, 1924, 29 (Easterwood Landmark); May 28, 1946 (Coleman's obituary); May 21, 1965 (Stella's obituary)
    Sanborn Maps, 1926, sheet 257; 1926/1950, sheet 257
    TGCAMB, November 1923, 29; December 1923, 29; February 1924, 28; April 1924, 34 (Jarman house)

176. **Harry T. Cruger House**
    TGCABM, May 1924, 27; June 1924, 34
    Waco City Directories, 1876–1928
    Sanborn Maps, 1926, sheet 294; 1926/1950, sheet 294
    US Census, 1860–1930

177. **Valentine and Kathleen Cox House**
    (Nabors-Cox House)
    TGCAMB, February 1923, 22 (Nabors); March 1925, 26; May 1925, 27 (Cox)
    Waco City Directories, 1921–22 to 1932–33
    US Census, 1940
    Sanborn Maps, 1926, sheet 257; 1926/1950, sheet 257

178. **John and Lucy Rowland House**
    (Rowland-Trice House)
    US Census, 1900–1940
    Sanborn Maps, 1926, sheet 244; 1926/1950, sheet 244
    TGCAMB, July 1929, 24 (prospective parsonage)
    Waco Tribune-Herald, October 7, 1934, 21 (Trice and Columbus Avenue Baptist)
    Waco News-Tribune, July 12, 1967 (E. L. Trice Sr.'s obituary)

179. **Charles Samuel and Regina Appell House**
    TGCAMB, October 1925, 17, 34
    Waco City Directories, 1921–22 to 1930–31
    US Census, 1920–1940
    Sanborn Maps, 1916, sheet 65; 1926, sheet 215
    WCCN II, 32

180. **Hafer-Dawson House**
    Waco City Directories, 1923–24 to 1939
    US Census, 1930, 1940
    Sanborn Maps, 1926, sheet 308; 1926/1950, sheet 308

181. **Chambers-Murphey-Kendrick House**
TGCAMB, October 1931, 20
Waco City Directories, 1919–20 to 1938
US Census, 1930, 1940
Waco News-Tribune, November 3, 1932, 5;
   December 23, 1937, 7
Waco Tribune-Herald, November 13, 1932, 13; July 8,
   2021, B2 (Dorothy's obituary)
Sanborn Map, 1926/1950, sheet 294

182. **Carl and Elsie Wallerstedt House**
Blueprints in possession of current owners
Waco City Directories, 1932–33 to 1948
US Census, 1920, 1940
Sanborn Map, 1926/1950, sheet 318
Waco News-Tribune, February 3, 1933, 4; June 1, 1933,
   7; November 2, 1933, 12
Carl A. Wallerstedt, *The Second Generation*
   (Waco: Wallerstedt, 1976), 110–33

183. **Washington Terrace Apartments**
TGCAMB, October 1928, 33
Waco News-Tribune, January 27, 1929, 28, 30;
   January 29, 1929, 32
Waco City Directories, 1930–31 to 1939
US Census, 1930, 1940
Sanborn Map, 1926/1950, sheet 201

184. **Charles and Clothilde Eubank House**
Waco City Directories, 1936–39
US Census, 1940
Sanborn Map, 1926/1950, sheet 318

185. **T. Walter and Eula Harrell House**
US Census, 1930, 1940
Waco City Directories, 1941, 1943
Waco News-Tribune, February 3, 1939
Waco Tribune-Herald, November 10, 1940, 18
   (Bible study)
Sanborn Map, 1926/1950, sheet 318
Maurie D. McInnis, "Scarlett Doesn't Live Here
   Anymore: Tara, *Gone with the Wind*, and the
   Southern Landscape Tradition," in *American
   Material Culture and the Texas Experience: The
   David B. Warren Symposium*, ed. Christine
   Waller Manca (Houston: Museum of Fine
   Arts, Houston, Bayou Bend Collection and
   Gardens, 2011), 2:94–121

Chapter Four. Tudor Revival

186. **Walter and Ida King House**
Waco City Directories, 1888–89 to 1923–24
US Census, 1920–1940
Waco News-Tribune, April 18, 1923, 8; May 25, 1924, 29
TGCAMB, May 1923, 15
Sanborn Maps, 1926, sheet 308; 1926/1950, sheet 308

187. **Howard and Olga Herrick House**
Waco City Directories, 1917–18 to 1923–24
Sanborn Maps, 1926, sheet 316; 1926/1950, sheet 316
Waco News-Tribune, October 18, 1925, 17
US Census, 1930

188. **J. Bruton and Frances Orand House**
Waco City Directories, 1910 to 1923–24
TGCAMB, September 1925, 25; December 1925, 24;
   February 1926, 33
US Census, 1900–1940
Sanborn Maps, 1926, sheet 316; 1926/1950, sheet 316

189. **Wilton and Ethel Lanning House
(Lanning-Stevens House)**
Waco City Directories, 1923–65
US Census (Waco), 1920, 1930, 1940
Waco News-Tribune, February 20, 1959
   (Frank F. Freeman's obituary)
Framed blueprint in the house
Phone conversation with Wilton A. Lanning Jr.,
   December 20, 2017

190. **Nat and Mildred Tanenbaum House**
Waco City Directories, 1926–41
US Census, 1920–1940
Sanborn Map, 1926/1950, sheet 318

191. **Harlon and Clara Fentress House
(Fentress-Hoehn House)**
Sanborn Map, 1926/1950, sheet 318
US Census, 1930–1940
Waco City Directories, 1923–24 to 1939
Waco Tribune-Herald, October 3, 2006 (Clara's obituary)

192. **George and Lillie Liddell House**
TGCAMB, September 1924, 28; November 1933,
   12 (Liddell)
Sanborn Maps, 1926, sheet 257; 1926/1950, sheet 257
Waco City Directories, 1926–41
US Census, 1920–1940

**Chapter Five. Mediterranean and
Spanish Colonial Revival**

**193. Valley View, the Summer Residence of William Waldo
and Helen Cameron (later Art Center Waco)**

Waco City Directories, 1898–99 to 1923–24

US Census, 1900–1940 (Waco), 1900 (Buffalo, NY), 1930
and 1940 (New York, NY), 1940 (Palm Beach, FL), and
1950 (Ivy, Albemarle County, VA)

R. J. Tolson, *A History of Wm. Cameron & Co., Inc.*
(Waco: J. S. Barnett, circa 1923–25); copy in the Texas
Collection, Baylor University

Waco Times-Herald, May 1, 1900, 4; May 27, 1900, 16
(Rogers's obituary)

Buffalo News, January 13, 1901, 5 (Baird-Cameron
weddings)

Waco News-Tribune, April 2, 1922, 18 (photos of Cameron
houses)

Waco Morning News, February 5, 1912, 3 (first reception
at 1717 Austin)

Temple Daily Telegram, June 19, 1910, 6 (dance at Valley
View)

Waco Morning News, June 17, 1917, 27 (dance at Valley
View)

Waco News-Tribune, October 12, 1921, 5; October 23,
1921, 9; October 26, 1921, 5; October 27, 1921, 7; October 28, 1921, 5; November 4, 1921, 5; November 6, 1921,
29; November 9, 1921, 5 (Cotton Palace parties)

Waco News-Tribune, April 2, 1922, 18 (photos of 1717
Austin and old Valley View)

Austin Statesman, June 22, 1922, 1; June 25, 1922, 20

Waco Farm and Labor Journal, June 29, 1922, 4 (wedding
of William Waldo and Helen)

Waco News-Tribune, May 20, 1927, 6 (bridge party)

Waco News-Tribune, August 18, 1927, 5; September 20,
1927, 5 (swimming parties)

Waco News-Tribune, April 20, 1928, 16; April 21, 1928, 14
(barbecues for Cameron managers and seven hundred employees)

Waco News-Tribune, June 9, 1928, 1 (Chamber of
Commerce reception)

Waco News-Tribune, August 11, 1936, 5 (party at Valley
View)

Waco News-Tribune, October 20, 1939, 8 (W. W. Cameron
funeral)

"Waco Is Mourning the Sudden Passing of William
Cameron," Waco newspaper clipping in the Texas
Collection, Baylor University

Waco News-Tribune, December 6, 1940, 8 (Helen and
Everett wedding)

Waco News-Tribune, October 18, 1942, 14 (Helen Jones at
Valley View)

Monmouth Inquirer (Freehold, NJ), August 20, 1923, 1
(Faith Baird Cameron and Howard Cole marriage)

North Adams Transcript (MA), March 12, 1930, 7 (Faith
Baird Cameron and Howard Cole divorce)

Merton M. Wilner, *Niagara Frontier: A Narrative and
Documentary History* (Chicago: S. J. Clarke Publishing,
1931), 4:39–40 (Courtlandt and Eleanor Van Clief)

"Waco: An Artful Renovation," *Texas Architect*, March/
April 1976, 14–15

Carl Hoover, "Former Art Center of Waco Building
Facing Demolition without Rescuer," *Waco Tribune-
Herald*, March 1, 2019

Rick Bostwick, "Historic Cameron Home Ours to Save,"
Waco Tribune-Herald, July 17, 2022

194. Veterans Administration Hospital Staff Quarters

TGCAMB, June 1930, 26; February 1931, 11

Waco City Directory, 1932–33

Texas Writers' Project of the Works Project Administra-
tion, *Texas: A Guide to the Lone Star State* (New York:
Hastings House, 1940); reprinted as J. Frank Davis,
*The WPA Guide to Texas: The Federal Writers' Project
Guide to Texas*, with a new introduction by Don
Graham (Austin: Texas Monthly Press, 1986), 362.

Waco News-Tribune, January 7, 1941, 1 (Mary Gough
Rubin's obituary); March 19, 1958, 1 (Dr. Rubin's
obituary)

Cynthia Field, *The Nation Builds for Those Who Served:
An Introduction to the Architectural Heritage of the
Veterans Administration* (Washington, DC: Veterans Administration and National Building Museum,
1980), 23

Michael C. Quinn (with research by Peter Flagg Maxson),
National Register nomination for "Veterans Administration Hospital Historic District," February 7, 1994

195. Harry and Sadie Kestner House

Waco City Directories, 1910–36

US Census, 1920–1940

Waco Tribune-Herald, March 10, 1935, 7 (partnership)

Waco News-Tribune, September 16, 1936, 5 (tea)

Sanborn Map, 1926/1950, sheet 318

Blueprints owned by Henry W. Wright

196. **Herman and Carrie Cason House**
Waco City Directories, 1900–01 to 1945
Waco News-Tribune, March 18, 1929, 3 (Joseph F. Cason's obituary); November 22, 1941, 1 (Herman F. Cason's obituary)
Sanborn Map, 1926/1950, sheet 330
Dan K. Utley and James W. Steely, *Guided with a Steady Hand: The Cultural Landscape of a Rural Texas Park* (Waco: Baylor University Press, 1998), 51, 61

Chapter Six. Period Cottages

197. **Albert and Esther Gugenheim House (Gugenheim-Trautschold House)**
TGCAMB, April 1924, 27
Waco City Directories, 1923–24 to 1951
Sanborn Map, 1926, sheet 330
US Census, 1920–1940
Roy E. Lane, *A Short Explanation of the Church of Saint Francis, Souvenir of the Dedication of San Francis Church on Thanksgiving Day, November 26, 1931* (Waco: Kelley-Bone Printing, 1932), Texas Collection, Baylor University
Waco News Tribune, December 2, 1965, 1, 14 (Carl Trautschold's obituary)
Kelley, *The Handbook of Waco*, 269

198. **William and Lenora Duffel House**
Waco City Directory, 1923–24
US Census, 1930
Waco Tribune-Herald, October 14, 1934, 14
Waco News-Tribune, January 15, 1935, 5
Sanborn Map, 1926/1950, sheet 244
TGCAMB, July 1929, 24 (Columbus Ave Baptist Church—contemplated parsonage)

199. **William and Myrtle Eastland House**
Waco City Directories, 1917–18 to 1941
US Census Records, 1920–1940
TGCAMB, October 1925, 34
Waco News-Tribune, March 7, 1926, 17–18
Sanborn Maps, 1926, sheet 242; 1926/1950, sheet 242

200. **Henry and Johanna Pochyla House**
Waco City Directories, 1923–24 to 1928
US Census, 1920–1940
TGCAMB, May 1926, 26

201. **Michael and Ellen Hunt House**
US Census, 1920, 1930
Waco City Directories, 1926–41
TGCAMB July 1929, 24; September 1929, 33
Sanborn Map, 1926/1950, sheet 240
Waco News-Tribune, April 7, 1933, 12; September 29, 1933, 7; December 5, 1933, 5; December 24, 1933, 20; September 14, 1934, 8; October 22, 1935, 5; August 30, 1950, 12; February 16, 1951, 1; May 3, 1952, 2
Waco Tribune-Herald, June 10, 1934, 17; November 25, 1974, 2 (Michael Hunt Jr.'s obituary)
Waco News-Citizen, November 21, 1964, 6

202. **Jesse and Jewel Lancaster House (Lancaster-Cunningham-Nathan House)**
Waco City Directories, 1928–39
US Census, 1940
Sanborn Map, 1926/1950, sheet 318

203. **Graves and Alice Darby House**
Waco City Directories, 1928–39
TGCAMB, May 1935, 15
US Census, 1940
Sanborn Map, 1926/1950, sheet 318

204. **John and London Bashara House**
Waco City Directories, 1907–08 to 1941
US Census, 1910–1940

Chapter Seven. Later Alternatives

205. **Ira W. and Martha Seley House (Braswell-Seley House)**
US Census (Waco), 1940 and 1950 (Braswell and Seley)
Waco City Directories, 1941–64
Sanborn Map, 1926/1950, sheet 318
Waco Tribune-Herald, June 26, 1938, 33
Waco Tribune-Herald, September 2, 1977 (Winthrop Seley's obituary)
Waco Tribune-Herald, October 25, 2010 (Sara Seley Jones's obituary)

206. **Dr. Maurice C. and Lavonia Jenkins Barnes House**
Waco News-Tribune, June 8, 1948, 6 (move-in)
Waco Tribune-Herald, June 20, 1948, 37 (description of house); December 15, 1968, 48 (Warner at UT)
Lavonia Jenkins Barnes, *Early Homes of Waco and the People Who Lived in Them* (Waco: Texian Press, 1970), vii (Stripling foreword), 179–85 (McGregor house)

Baylor University Institute for Oral History, "Oral Memoirs of Lavonia Leverett Jenkins Barnes," Series 1, transcript, 72

Mark Robert Browning, "Recovering Provenance: Historic Preservation in Waco, 1953–1980" (master's thesis, Baylor University, 2010)

207. Mrs. Hattie Richards House

Waco City Directories, 1902–03 to 1923–24

"Chapel in the Woods: O'Neil Ford—A. B. Swank, Architects," *Pencil Points* 21, no. 2 (February 1940)

S. B. Zisman, "The Architect and the House 5: O'Neil Ford of Dallas, Texas," *Pencil Points* 21, no. 4 (April 1940)

Original blueprints (in possession of the owners)

208. George and Adele Bashara House

US Census, 1900–1940

Waco Tribune-Herald, September 15, 1940, 24; July 6, 1947, 19; December 30, 1951, 19

Waco News-Tribune, December 22, 1953, 12; October 4, 1955, 4; February 1, 1956, 7

209. Charles K. and Katherine Durham House (Durham-Buchanan-Morrow House)

Waco City Directories, 1921–22 to 1939

US Census, 1920–1940

Sanborn Maps, 1899, sheet 14, corner of Clifton (609); 1926, sheet 240 (Durham); 1926, sheet 212, corner of Barron (705, Lyons)

Larmour, *Architectural Waco*, 6

Waco News-Tribune, October 11, 1925, 18 (Durham); January 28, 1926, 5 (Compton-Durham wedding); February 10, 1926, 5 (Compton-Durham wedding); December 23, 1954, 13 (Hicks); January 26, 1955, 9; January 18, 1967, 1, 2 ("Pilgrimage")

Waco Tribune-Herald, July 9, 1950, 35 (Buchanan); January 5, 1958, 39 (Holloway); May 10, 1959, 1 (Holloway)

Oral history interview with E. B. "Eb" Morrow, by Kari Vanhoozer, June–July 1997, Baylor Institute for Oral History, interviews 13 and 14

Personal conversations with Eb Morrow, circa 2000–02

INDEX